ONE
BUT NOT THE
SAME

GOD'S DIVERSE KINGDOM COME
THROUGH RACE, CLASS AND GENDER

CHRIS WILLIAMSON
FOREWORD BY TOBYMAC

WESTBOW
PRESS

WestBow Press™
1663 Liberty Drive
Bloomington, IN 47403
www.westbowpress.com
Phone: (866) 928-1240

All Scripture references and quotes unless otherwise noted are
from the New King James Version of the Holy Scriptures.

First published by WestBow Press 12/21/09

ISBN: 978-1-4497-0009-6 (sc)
ISBN: 978-1-4497-0010-2 (e)
ISBN: 978-1-4497-0011-9 (hc)

Library Congress of Control Number: 2009942836

Printed in the United States of America
Bloomington, Indiana

This book is printed on acid-free paper.

DEDICATION

This book is dedicated to the memory of Peggy Southard, a woman of God who loved and prayed me into the community of Franklin and the work of planting a multidimensional church. I proudly credit Peggy, who went home to be with Jesus in 2007 after heroically battling cancer, and her husband Stu as the reason for losing my record contract when I arrived in Nashville, Tennessee in 1992! They fervently prayed for a black man to come up the road to Franklin, Tennessee and serve the entire community as a bridge building, gospel preaching change agent. It was their prayers that helped awaken me to God's plan for my life to plant a church that would reflect the splendor of heaven on earth.

Peggy and Stu exemplified God's Diverse Kingdom through how they lived and served. So often they put their time and money where their hearts were by investing in people and efforts in our city that fostered the holistic empowerment of the underserved. When an older African American woman in our city needed help learning how to read, it was Peggy who helped her. I watched as the Southard family took in two African American children from the community in a time of great family crisis. Peggy mentored many women of all ages, classes, and races. She poured into my wife Dorena when she had complications birthing our fourth child. As a young pastor, I will never forget how Peggy would encourage me and call my name. I can still hear her voice encouraging me to rest in the grace and power of Jesus.

Peggy's favorite song was "In Christ Alone". I can see her now in heaven with arms stretched to Jesus in triumphant worship surrounded by her brothers and sisters from every tribe, language, people, and nation. The glorious diversity of heaven did not shock Peggy when she arrived there. She lived on earth what she now enjoys in heaven. I was blessed to officiate her home going service in the church she helped pray into existence. The church was full of people from all walks of life. Many different hues and cultures were in attendance to celebrate the privilege of knowing her. When the singing, dancing, preaching, rejoicing, and crying were over, God brought many people into the kingdom that day through saving faith in Jesus Christ. Peggy's legacy of love will continue to live on through her family, her friends, her pastor, her church, and now this book.

GDK Come,

Pastor Chris

"No guilt in life, no fear in death, this is the power of Christ in me. From life's first cry to final breath, Jesus commands my destiny. No power of hell, no scheme of man can ever pluck me from His hand. 'Til He returns or calls me home here in the power of Christ I'll stand!"

Lyrics from "In Christ Alone" written by
Stuart Townend and Keith Getty

Contents

FOREWORD
By TobyMac

I remember when I first met Chris on the campus of Liberty University in 1987. He reminded me of the rapper LL Cool J because he had his east coast thing going on with his Kangol hat and striped Adidas. Chris came off kind of hardcore, and besides playing basketball, I didn't think we had much in common. But one day while sitting around with a bunch of students between classes in the Demos Hall, Chris and I discovered we did in fact have something in common. We both loved to rap! With the crowd swelling and our friend Moose on the beat box, Chris and I would kick rhymes to the people's applause.

At the spur of the moment we decided to put together a rap group called Revelation. Back then Chris was known as "D-vine MC" and my rap name was "DC Talk". We were joined in the group by another black guy named Barry "Suave" Lyons and a white kid named Todd "MC T" Peck. Together we made one song and one appearance during halftime at a Liberty basketball game. Little did we know that this multi-racial rap group would be a picture of both of our lives and legacies going forward.

I went on from Revelation to form another group on campus with Kevin Max Smith and Michael Tait and we called it "DC Talk". Chris joined up with some brothers and they launched "Transformation Crusade", a rap group committed to straight up, inner city evangelism. Eventually DC Talk moved to Nashville and began to tour extensively. God blessed me to live on stage night after night with Kevin and Mike and share about the blessed diversity we enjoyed off stage. We didn't think about our contrasts until other people started asking us questions about how we got along.

When Chris came to Nashville in 1992 we didn't get a chance to spend much time together. I later heard that he was working at Christ Community Church in Franklin, Tennessee. A couple of years later, Chris started a multi-racial church in Franklin called Strong Tower Bible Church. We were pulling for each other because this was around the same time I launched Gotee Records. I wanted Gotee Records to reflect God's rich diversity in every way through the wide range of artists we would go on to sign. In addition, Chris and I were fortunate to labor in a non-profit organization DC Talk founded in 1995 called the ERACE Foundation. ERACE stands for Eliminating Racism And Creating Equality and Chris is one of the board members.

Pastor Chris and I both have hearts to build and experience God's Diverse Kingdom right here and right now. We're joined at the hip on that. I'm blessed to be doing it through my family, friends, ministry, and band "Diverse City". Pastor Chris is doing it through Strong Tower Bible Church, his speaking, and this book. You will find these pages to be full of biblical truths, balanced perspectives, and powerful challenges to heed. I can assure you that Pastor Chris is living what he so honestly writes about in this book. God has blessed him to talk about painful things in our past and present history without the anger or the empty rhetoric. He is a voice that must be heard and this is a book that must be read. You probably won't agree with everything Pastor Chris writes, but isn't that the beauty of diversity? God expects us to be one without having to be the same.

I believe that God is a creative artist and as a body we are more beautiful together than divided. We will never truly be a city on a hill until we are in fact a diverse city. You don't have to wait to go to heaven before you can experience the beauties of God's Diverse Kingdom. God wants you to pray for and live in that kingdom right now, but you will only experience this kingdom to the degree that you are willing to lose your life in order to find it (Matthew 10:39). Only in your loss will there be gain. Only in your dying to self will there be a resurrection. Only in your surrender will there be victory. Therefore, I encourage you to jump in with both feet as you keep this in mind: We are once choice from together.

One Love,

TobyMac

INTRODUCTION:
THE KINGDOM OF GOD IS AT HAND!

*"But if I cast out demons by the Spirit of God, surely the
kingdom of God has come upon you."* Matthew 12:28

The first and only time I heard Evangelist Tom Skinner speak was in 1993 at
a Christian Community Development Association conference. I was twenty-
five years old and full of enthusiasm. I was fresh on my job with Franklin
Community Ministries in Franklin, Tennessee as their pastoral intern for
urban ministry. I had never heard of Tom Skinner before but I soon found
out why so many people loved and admired this former chaplain of the
Washington Redskins. Tom was a one-time gangbanger turned preacher.
In the racially charged climate of the 1960's he was a rare combination of
evangelical thought married to radical social activism. Tom Skinner was
black, free, and outspoken.

On this day in my hometown of Baltimore, Maryland, Reverend Skinner
stood grasping a small, metal lectern that looked like a toothpick in his
large hands. I'll never forget it. His first word to the audience was simply,
"Kingdom". That's all he said. After a brief pause, he used his large wingspan
to illustrate length and breadth. With everyone paying full attention, he went
on to say, "Kingdom. It is the King's dominion." For the next two hours
and without a Bible in his hand, Tom Skinner preached one of the most
thorough, biblical expositions I had ever heard on any subject. I had never
seen anything like this. Not only was I caught up with his flawless homiletics,
I was also captured by his content. After the conference ended I went back to
Tennessee knowing that I had witnessed something very unusual.

The following year at the age of 52, Tom Skinner went home to be with Jesus
after battling leukemia. His wife Barbara continued his work of developing
leaders, knocking down walls of discrimination, and raising consciousness. I

am blessed to have had the privilege of hearing this unsung, spiritual giant. That initial seed of the kingdom would sit in me dormant until now.

BOOKER T. WASHINGTON'S HAND ILLUSTRATION

God has a way of catapulting leaders from the fetters of obscurity and onto the national stage of human progress at precisely the right time. One such person was Booker T. Washington. Booker T. Washington is considered by many to be the first national spokesman for black people in America. Climbing up from the doldrums of slavery to make monumental strides in the field of education, Booker T. Washington was the champion black people desperately needed. He was also the black man that white people faithfully trusted. He merged the black and white worlds even within his own racial make up. He had the ability to communicate to both sides with wisdom and experience. In his landmark speech at the Atlanta Exposition of 1895, Washington was given the task of speaking to thousands of whites and blacks on hand. If he were too accommodating the black masses would despise him. If he were too militant the white power base would reject him, thus shutting down access to relationships necessary for progress.

As he wrote in his autobiography Up From Slavery, Washington encouraged blacks and whites in this speech to work together by casting down their buckets in the sea of one another's resources. He said, "In all things that are purely social we can be as separate as the fingers, yet one as the hand in all things essential to mutual progress." (p. 107) Booker T. Washington believed blacks and whites didn't have to live together in order to work together. He didn't feel there was a reason for blacks and whites to socialize. With his illustration about the hand, Booker T. Washington said what many white people in the south believed but didn't say. He said what the majority of black people wanted to say but couldn't say. His message may have been palatable and even necessary on the eve of the 20th century in southern America, but it was not right. Unfortunately, Christianity had lost its voice in this area of social integration because the churches were leading the way in racial division. America would stay legally and socially separated until 1954. This was the year the Supreme Court banned "separate but equal" segregation in public schools through the landmark Brown vs. the Board of Education case. This ruling paved the way for other legislation to be passed like the Civil Rights Act of 1964 and the Voting Rights Act of 1965. These Acts reinforced the 14th and 15th Amendments to the United States Constitution, and helped move America towards a more equal and integrated society.

What Booker T. Washington missed was that our fingers may be separate but they work together as one unit at all times. Our fingers can't pick and choose when they want to be together or work together. They have no such choice. When impulses and dictates from the brain channel through electrons in our central nervous system, our five fingers, if we are fortunate to have them all, work together as one. Each finger has a role. The thumb, the pointing finger, the middle finger, the ring finger, and the pinkie finger each has a specific part to play. A hand can function without any one of its fingers, but it doesn't function as well.

THE HAND ON THE COVER OF THE BOOK

When we look at our hands they have a way of telling a portion of our story. The hand on the cover of this book is symbolic of many things. First, it represents our unity working within our diversity, and our diversity working within our unity. You cannot truly have unity without diversity or diversity without unity. The different colors on the fingertips speak to the racial uniqueness we each have through our Creator, Jesus Christ (Colossians 1:15-16). God has got the whole world in His hands! Red, brown, yellow, black, and white, we are precious in His sight! Through Christ, we are all one but not the same.

Secondly, by looking at the hand on the cover you don't know if it is a hand belonging to a wealthy person or an impoverished person. We must all bear in mind that we came into the world naked and without anything in our hands. There were no inherited rings on our fingers or dirt under our fingernails from working in the fields. We came out of the womb crying with our empty hands reaching up towards heaven. Our hands should be in the same posture now, reaching up to God. One day, hopefully not soon, we will die with empty hands. Our hands will not carry in them any of the riches or material things we accumulated or lost over our lifetime. Our hands won't carry the pride of wealth or the shame and stress associated with extreme poverty, sickness, or unemployment. In heaven, our hands won't beg from other hands any more. But on earth, the hands of the rich and the poor are to mutually empower, protect, and provide for one another until Jesus returns.

Finally, if you take another look at the hand on the cover you will not be able to discern what gender the hand is. Is it a man's hand or a woman's hand? Because of how we are trained and conditioned, the first inclination many of us have is to automatically assume the hand on the cover is a man's hand. It very well could be, but once again in the spirit of diversity, it could be a woman's hand, too. Everyone looks at things through the lens of their experiences. There are obvious differences between a man and a woman, most of which are physical in nature. But as we will see in this book, Jesus Christ's personal example and teachings addressed not only the sins of sexism, but racism and classism in addition. There is to be no place for any of these vices in the Diverse Kingdom of God.

AN EVENTFUL SEVEN DAYS

Jesus said, *"If I cast out demons by the power of God then the kingdom of God has come upon you"* (Matthew 12:28). God's Diverse Kingdom is coming upon us and we should desire it more than anything else in the world. I want God's presence and His power to work in me, through me, and around me. When His kingdom comes, abundant life and joy unspeakable come as a result. There's never a dull moment in the kingdom. Let me do my best to explain to you how God's Diverse Kingdom came upon me in the past seven days:

Thursday: At noon I attended a "Synago" prayer meeting for pastors in our city. Synago is a Greek word meaning "come together". Synago creates opportunities for pastors in our city to periodically worship and work together in the power of the Holy Spirit to the end that God is glorified, unity is modeled, and needs are met. We alternate churches when we pray and eat together twice a month. On Thursday evening I attended a banquet to support a ministry to Native Americans called the Red Road. I was once again reminded of the tragedies and triumphs of the First Nations people. My Executive Pastor John Maguire humbly repented before Charles Robinson, a member of the Choctaw nation. Pastor John shared how one of His Irish ancestors sailed with Columbus. John said to the audience that had a majority of white people in attendance, "It may not have been your fault, but you must ask God, is it now my responsibility?'"

Friday: I went to a local high school football game and met up with my good friend Steve Berger. Steve is the pastor of Grace Chapel in Leiper's Fork. We make it a priority to hang out together on a regular basis. Between quarters of the game we discussed our pulpit swap and joint worship service our churches will have together in December. I love this man with all of my heart.

Sunday: Richard Twiss of the Lakota tribe spoke in our church. He brought a challenging word about our narrowness and self-absorption as American Christians. Charles and Siouxsan Robinson worshiped God through a historic Native dance while wearing full regalia. Our ethnically mixed choir sang the songs of glory, and we heard a stunning selection from Grammy award winner and member of the Mohican tribe, Bill Miller. We placed huge boxes at the doors and collected shoes for orphans to be distributed around the world through Soles for Souls. In the same worship service we prayed over Mike and Susann Mayernick about their upcoming adoption of a beautiful Ugandan girl named Josie. The Mayernick's previously adopted two African American boys into their family of four, giving them a blessed coalition of white, African American, and now African. Their family is one of several families in our church that represents the Diverse Kingdom of God through multi-ethnic adoption.

Tuesday: I attended our church's staff meeting and joyfully counted the shoes that were brought to church. Our goal was to collect 1,000 pairs so we stopped counting at 1,100! My staff is comprised of the most outstanding men and women you will ever find. By ethnic break down we have four African American males, two Caucasian males, two African American women, and two Caucasian women. In addition we have one Mexican American woman and one bi-racial male, and these two are married to each other.

Wednesday: I read two more chapters of the book <u>Same Kind of Different as Me</u> by Ron Hall and Denver Moore. It's a book about two men who came together from two extremely different worlds racially, culturally, and economically. My wife Dorena and her good friend Sherri Gragg (who happens to be a precious white sister) are teaching through this book in one of our Christian Education classes. On Wednesday evening I taught a diverse group of men in our Apollos Training Institute (ATI). We had special guests from Ghana, the Congo, and Malawi join us for class. I asked each of the men to pray for us in his native tongue. Once again God gave us a glimpse of heaven. We were reminded afresh that our God is global.

Thursday: In the morning I met with my pastors and elders to discuss and pray through crucial church matters. My elders are men who range in age, occupation, economic classification, and past denominational experience. By ethnic breakdown we have six African Americans and four Caucasian Americans on our team. At noon, I attended a luncheon for pastors at my friend Rick White's church. Rick pastors the People's Church in Franklin and he is considered one of our city's spiritual fathers. Rick informed us how his church is active serving in the African country of Malawi. He invited this group of pastors to join him in the work. Back at the office I received an email from Mark DeYmaz of Mosaic Church in Central Arkansas informing me about a gathering over the Internet of key leaders in the multi-ethnic church movement. I studied to preach my second sermon from the letter of Philemon and I also prepared to speak to a group of millionaires on Saturday night called the Buffalo Bills. The Bills are coming to town to play our beloved Titans.

On Thursday evening I went to a banquet at Fellowship Bible Church for a ministry our church supports called African Leadership. I heard once again how founder and director Larry Warren and his team of Africans and Americans are training pastors in twenty-two different countries on the continent of Africa. The African church needs spiritual and biblical depth and African Leadership provides that assistance through a curriculum called Bible Training Center for Pastors (BTCP). African Leadership also ministers to Africans in the throes of famine, the aids epidemic, drought, starvation, and the emerging onslaught of Islam. Larry told the audience that one of the Islamic leaders that he and I ministered to in Darfur 5 years ago now has a son in BTCP classes and a daughter in the local Christian school. At the banquet I sat next to some old friends, Brandon and Darlene Dyson. Brandon was one of my first elders when we planted the church in 1995. He was born in Nigeria and he likes to say he is a true African American even though he is white! Brandon, Darlene and their six children, including two from Sierra Leone, are still an intricate part of our fellowship. Darlene and one of our ladies named Jodi Clark are active in serving and bringing awareness about widows and orphans in Sudan. I left the banquet energized about what God is doing in Africa!

This was my life in just seven days! I am blessed and humbled to see God's Diverse Kingdom come in my midst. I am so thankful that God would include me in what He's doing. And the amazing thing is that God is poised to do so much more! He has a way of doing exceedingly, abundantly, above all that we could ever ask or imagine (Ephesians 3:20). Like the late Tom Skinner, I have made a commitment to God that as I go about teaching and preaching His Word I will not fail to introduce people to the kingdom of God. Whether in person or through this book, my message will be like the ones John the Baptist and Jesus Christ delivered to their original audiences when they said, *"Repent, for the* (diverse) *kingdom of God is at hand!"* (Matthew 3:2, 4:17; "diverse" added)

CONSIDERATION: GRASPING THE KINGDOM CONCEPT

You can tell what's on a person's heart by what they talk about all of the time. For instance, men who are in love and happily married talk about their wives to anyone who will listen. Moms talk about their kids to the point of bragging. Business people talk about the world of business and finance as if they actually lived on Wall Street. Politicians talk about politics, especially during an election year. Sports fans talk about sports anywhere and anytime. Singers enjoy talking about music, and Jesus Himself spoke a great deal about *"the kingdom of heaven"*.

If you've ever noticed, the topic of the kingdom was at the forefront of Jesus' teaching and preaching. He began His earthly ministry by saying, *"Repent, for the kingdom of heaven is at hand"* (Matthew 4:17). He ended His earthly ministry at the Last Supper by telling the disciples He would not drink of the fruit of the vine again until the day when He drinks it anew with them in His Father's kingdom (Matthew 26:29). After being arrested in the Garden of Gethsemane Jesus told the Roman governor Pilate that He was in fact a king and that His kingdom was not of this world because if it were, His servants would fight to keep Him from being crucified (John 18:36-37). The kingdom abounded in the heart of Jesus so no wonder it came out of His mouth repeatedly (Matthew 12:34).

Jesus would regularly use the phrase, *"The kingdom of heaven is like…"* and then He would go on to use several earthly illustrations, also known as parables, to communicate divine truths to His listeners. Jesus used images of children, seeds, a dragnet, a pearl of great price, leaven, and hidden treasure to name a few. The disciples would begin to grasp *"the mysteries of the kingdom"* by asking Him to explain in private what He proclaimed in public (Matthew 13:10-11). By doing this, the disciples showed that they were hungry and thirsty for righteousness, and they were willing to dig for wisdom as for silver (Proverbs 2:4-5). When Jesus spoke about the kingdom, many people in the crowd simply walked away bewildered or hardened, being content to sink deeper into spiritual ignorance and apathy.

"The kingdom" is one of those terms that Christians use all of the time but many of us can't explain exactly what it means because it is a grand and somewhat illusive concept. As with anything biblical, the context helps determine the definition. The challenge with deciphering the kingdom is that Jesus mentions it in several different ways. For instance, Jesus tells us to seek the kingdom of God first and not material things (Matthew 6:33). He told a group of adults that the only way to receive the kingdom was by becoming like a little child (Matthew 18:1-4). The Bible says we can inherit the kingdom (Matthew 25:34), see the kingdom (John 3:3), enter the kingdom (John 3:5), and wait on the kingdom (Luke 23:51). Jesus taught us that the kingdom of God is near us (Luke 10:9) and it is coming (Matthew 16:28). This means the kingdom is both now and not yet. The kingdom is in us, that is, in our midst (Luke 17:21), and it is in heaven (Matthew 7:21). The kingdom of heaven is the kingdom of God. The kingdom of God is the kingdom of Jesus (Luke 23:42). It is both a place to live and a way to live (Romans 14:17).

THE KINGDOM IN SIMPLEST FORM

The kingdom of God that Jesus told us to pray for, look for, and live out in its simplest form is the reign of God, namely, the reign of Jesus Christ over everything, every place, and every one (Luke 1:31-33). The kingdom is all about King Jesus exercising His dominion over every domain, whether visible or invisible, earthly or eternal. In heaven, everyone and everything submits to God and obeys Him without question. Heaven comes to earth when God's people submit to this King and obey Him without hesitation. We are to bow everything to King Jesus—our hearts, minds, wills, bodies, plans, and resources. We are to also bow our fears, limitations, burdens, perplexities, and shortcomings to Him. He alone is capable of taking them, dealing with them, and transforming us in the process by His abundant grace. The King's dominion occurs when we allow Jesus' person, power, passion, and principles to daily dominate every detail of our lives. This is why with passion we preach the need for men and women everywhere to repent and turn to Jesus because the return of God is imminent (Acts 3:19-20, Revelation 21:7, 12). Jesus is coming again and when He returns He will rule and reign forever (Revelation 22:1-5).

The kingdom is not only the reign and return of Jesus Christ, but it is also the reach of God. As you will see later in this book, whenever John the Baptist or Jesus preached "the gospel of the kingdom" it was always accompanied with hands-on, mercy ministry to the poor, diseased, and disenfranchised. Jesus said, *"And this gospel of the kingdom will be preached in all the world as a witness to all the nations, and then the end will come"* (Matthew 24:14). Unbelievers from all nations should witness the gospel through our words and our works. The rule of King Jesus and His merciful heart is realized in how He calls people discarded to the outside to join Him on the inside (Matthew 22:1-10). Whether those people are poor, maimed, lame, and blind, Jesus has room for them in His house and at His table (Luke 14:15-24). Like King David with Jonathan's son Mephibosheth, Jesus gives the physically and spiritually crippled the best seats at the table (II Samuel 9:1-13). Jesus invites people to the table that religious people feel shouldn't even be in the same room with Him (Luke 7:36-50). Let's not make the same pompous mistake. If we are not actively reaching and touching underserved people in our families, communities, and around the world we have missed the message, ministry, and model of Jesus Christ, the One we claim to follow, emulate, and imitate. There's no time for empty, vain religion (James 1:27) because Jesus is coming.

God's mercy towards us should motivate us to reach out to others the way He reached down to us. Because of God's great love He transferred us out of spiritual darkness and into the kingdom of light (Colossians 1:13), causing us to be His royal, and hopefully loyal subjects. This translation from dark to light places us immediately into spiritual war with the kingdom of Satan (Luke 11:18). As a result, the subjects of God's kingdom suffer both spiritual and physical violence (Matthew 11:12) while still maintaining our blessed position as conquerors (Romans 8:37). This is the kingdom mindset. The kingdom mind is a victorious mind (I Corinthians 15:57), a triumphant mind (II Corinthians 2:14), a focused mind (Colossians 3:1-4), and an aggressive mind (II Corinthians 10:3-6). We know that all beings whether angelic or human do not currently acknowledge this kingship of Jesus Christ, which is why He will return personally in the future to establish His rule on the earth from Jerusalem (Revelation 1:7, 12:10; Micah 4:1-7). In the meantime He has placed His church in the world and has authorized it as His primary agent to represent His kingdom, His name, and His interests until Christ returns (Ephesians 1:22-23).

THE KINGDOM IN RELATION TO THE CHURCH

For Jewish people of old, thoughts of the kingdom went hand-in-hand with expectations of the coming Messiah. The Jews were anticipating a Messiah who would deliver them nationally from Rome and re-establish them as a mighty force on the earth that would be in subjection to no one but God (Acts 1:6), but Jesus' ministry as Messiah was first a matter of spiritual deliverance. He came as a Lamb to be slain in order to deliver Jews as well as Gentiles from the penalty of sin, which is eternal death (Isaiah 53:7, John 1:29). Jesus delivered us by dying on the cross in our stead and rising from the dead three days later (I Corinthians 15:3-4). Jesus ascended to heaven on a cloud (Acts 1:9-11) and will return to earth in the future as a Lion bent on conquering and reigning (Genesis 49:9-10, II Thessalonians 1:3-10, Revelation 5:5, 19:15). In trying to understand how God works we can ascertain that the spiritual always precedes the physical, and the spiritual is always greater than the physical (II Corinthians 4:18). This is why the Jews by and large missed Jesus at His first coming (John 1:9) and this is why many Christians miss Jesus in the church today. We are too physical or carnal minded and we keep attempting to see and grasp spiritual things in the flesh.

Nevertheless, Jesus spoke about "the kingdom" long before He ever mentioned the paradigm of "the church", and He spoke more times about the kingdom than He ever spoke about the church. Why is it that we tend to do the opposite and talk more about the church than we do the kingdom? It may be because the kingdom calls for repentance whereas the church calls for members. The kingdom calls for humility and brokenness whereas the church foolishly calls for legalistic perfection. The kingdom thrives on hope but the church often conjures up fear. The church is content with sameness but the kingdom calls for oneness expressing itself through diversity. Those in seminary are typically taught how to plant churches but not how to build the kingdom. Pastors tend to go after pew members and not kingdom people. I have learned the hard way that the pew warmers are usually my biggest headaches whereas kingdom people are my biggest assets. Kingdom people aren't waiting to cast the first stone at brothers and sisters caught in sin. They are too busy hurling stones at modern day Goliaths that are threatening the advancement of God's Diverse Kingdom.

Church has to be more than just a place to herd people in once or twice a week. Church should no longer play on our natural desires to be safe and comfortable. The kingdom must be preached because it challenges and stretches us to grow spiritually even if that means we must suffer to do so (II Thessalonians 1:5). Church tends to be about us, whereas the kingdom is all about Jesus. The notion of church, at least the way we do it nowadays, is easier to participate in and get a hold of, whereas the kingdom is somewhat nebulous, obscure, and ever changing. This is why we leave it alone. We remain churchy because we can't reduce the kingdom to three points and a poem or seven easy steps. It is not until we begin to grapple and wrestle with spiritual truths about God's ways that we will hear Jesus say, *"You are not far from the kingdom of God"* (Mark 12:34).

The kingdom and the church are not the same but they are intertwined, related, and even inseparable. Jesus couldn't talk about the church without mentioning the kingdom. The word "church" is found only three times in the gospels and all three occurrences are recorded in Matthew's gospel (Matthew 16:18, 18:17), whereas the word "kingdom" is found 54 times in Matthew alone. When Jesus introduced the model of the church to Peter in Matthew 16:13-19, He mentioned the kingdom in the same breath with it. Jesus said the church He would build would be given *"the keys of the kingdom"* to bind and to loose the spiritual gates of hell. Keys signify power and authority because keys have the ability to lock and unlock doors or gates; therefore, if the church is the people, the kingdom is the power (I Corinthians 4:20).

This means that if individual Christians and churches don't begin to understand the unequalled power of the kingdom that God has placed at our disposal, then we will continue to be powerless, irrelevant, and of low impact in today's society. For just as there are laws that govern the natural world, there are laws that govern the spiritual world. Kingdom people believe God's laws work even when things don't look so good or make sense to the naked eye. Like the law of gravity in nature, kingdom laws in the spirit realm concerning giving, loving, and forgiving work when they are applied. We have tried to be the church without understanding the implications of the kingdom. Conversely, we must beware of modern day movements that emphasize the kingdom to the exclusion of the local church. These misinformed zealots do this because they have been either burned by or burned out with the church as an institution. The truth is, there is no kingdom without the local church and there is no effective local church without the laws of the kingdom operating in and through the people of God.

Today's Christianity, especially in the west, has by and large become "churchanity". We are continuing to find out that church isn't working the way it's supposed to work for saved people on the inside or for lost people on the outside. God's people are entering the culture of church at a faster rate than they are entering the kingdom of God (Matthew 21:31-32), and not everyone who enters the church will enter the kingdom (Matthew 7:21-23). We know church and our traditions, but we don't always know and apply the truths of the kingdom. We stand strong for our denominational distinctions, and that has its place, but we usually have little conviction for the kingdom. We read right over those passages in the Bible causing us to be content, remaining a part of churches and Christian ministries that don't operate or look anything like the kingdom of heaven Jesus spoke about, personally modeled, and told us to pray for that it might invade earth.

A DIVERSE CITY

In the Sermon on the Mount, Jesus compared His followers to being *"a city that is set on a hill"* (Matthew 5:14). He used this illustration because the city of Jerusalem sat up on a hill (Mark 10:32-33). Jerusalem used a lot of limestone for its architecture, so when lights from torches and lamps cascaded against the white stones in the darkest of night, the city would "light up" and it could be seen from miles around. Disciples of Jesus are the light of the world (Matthew 5:14) and we make up the residency of this city on a hill. Jesus wants His spiritually adopted sons and daughters from all nations and walks of life to be elevated and seen in the midst of this dark, crooked, and perverse generation (Philippians 2:15). People living in darkness need to see the city's lights so that they can ultimately meet the Light of the city, Jesus Christ (Isaiah 9:2, Revelation 21:23).

This city on a hill is here on earth right now through the church, which is the bride of Christ (John 3:29, Ephesians 5:23-32). We are also told from the Scriptures that a city will come down from heaven in the future and it will be called *"the New Jerusalem"* (Revelation 21:2). The apostle John also calls this city *"the bride, the Lamb's wife"* (Revelation 21:9-11), and it is comprised of people from various nations and ethnic groups (Revelation 21:24). A "diverse city" is coming down from heaven like a bride coming down the aisle to her husband. Do you see her? This means the *"city on a hill"* in Matthew 5:14 is the same city as *"the New Jerusalem"* in Revelation 21:2 because both are descriptions of the one bride of Christ. So guess what? Christ's bride is a racially mixed, economically mixed, and gender mixed bride. This means that Jesus is in a mixed marriage!

That's beautiful and it should make us shout, but there is an obvious disconnect that should also make us weep, and here it is: The kingdom of God on earth through the church appears to be theoretical at best because the city coming from heaven is diversified whereas the city going to heaven is by and large homogenized in its local expressions. In other words, we don't look like where we're going. Our churches within *the* Church and our spiritual cities within *the* City are sadly segregated and separated along racial and denominational lines. We all know that no segregated and separated church is going to have a lasting impact on a diverse world. It's past time for the church, or should I say the kingdom of God on earth, to come together and be united in the midst of our diversity. We are much more potent and successful when we come together under the banner of Jesus. We are much more reflective of heaven and God's great love when we come together as one.

YOUR "DIVERSE" KINGDOM COME

In the same Sermon on the Mount Jesus taught His disciples how to pray and one aspect of that tutorial was for His followers to pray, *"Your kingdom come. Your will be done on earth as it is in heaven"* (Matthew 6:10). As we discovered, the kingdom of God is the reign of Christ, the return of Christ, and the reach of Christ, but it is also the redeemed of Christ. Jesus will soon return from heaven with a diverse throng of saints He personally redeemed (Revelation 19:11-16). Therefore, God's reign, return, and reach are to be represented every day and every way through His redeemed sons and daughters in the earth.

To know what's coming from heaven we need to know what's in heaven. If we were to fast-forward once again to Revelation 5:9, we would see that the Lamb has succeeded in redeeming us by His blood to God from *"every tribe and tongue and people and nation."* Heaven is obviously not segregated but wondrously diversified. Therefore to pray for the Father's kingdom to come from heaven to earth is to pray for diversity to come from heaven to earth because the Father's coming kingdom is a Diverse Kingdom. It is a Diverse City full of wonderful diversity and the good news is that we don't have to wait to get to heaven to experience it. According to Jesus we can have this Diverse Kingdom today just like we can have other aspects of the Lord's prayer such as provision for our felt needs, forgiveness from sin, and deliverance from evil today. If we truly want diversity we can have it now. Only as we allow the Spirit of Jesus to work in us to want what He wants (Philippians 2:13) will this happen. If you don't want to see, acknowledge, or experience this Diverse Kingdom it reveals that you have been tragically misinformed and sadly denied in your Christian upbringing and experience. You didn't think heaven would be full of people who look and act like just you, did you? There is no better time than now to step out of ignorance and into the light of truth.

And the truth is, wherever Jesus goes diversity is supposed to follow. Regretfully, that doesn't always play itself out among the people of God. Wherever we go homogeneous expression seems to follow. In America, black

Christians keep hanging with black Christians and white believers continue fellowshipping with white believers. Wealthy Christians continue to engage with other rich believers, and city churches rarely cross over the county line to worship and work with suburban churches. We do this because we like to be with people who are like us. It's comfortable from a racial, economic, cultural, and denominational standpoint. However, we understand from the Scriptures that God's Diverse Kingdom is comprised of people from various ethnicities, all classes, and both genders. The apostle Paul put it this way, *"There is neither Jew nor Greek* (RACE)*, there is neither slave nor free* (CLASS)*, there is neither male nor female* (GENDER)*; for you are all one in Christ Jesus"* (Galatians 3:28; Parenthesis added).

The premise of this book is built upon God's layout of diversity and oneness found in Galatians 3:28. We must bear in mind that this verse does not magically erase or deny ethnic, economic, or gender distinctions in the body of Christ. It simply celebrates and encourages unity in the presence of diversity. Paul wrote this to prove we can be one without having to be the same, just like the Godhead. God is one in His essence (Deuteronomy 6:4, I Timothy 2:5), yet plural and distinct in Person (Ephesians 2:18). The Father is not the Son and the Son is not the Holy Spirit, yet these three are one God. This mystery is called the "trinity" and it can't be adequately explained or fully understood—yet it is true. I Timothy 3:16 says, *"And without controversy great is the mystery of godliness: God was manifested in the flesh…"* When Jesus walked the earth He was mysteriously 100% God and 100% man. This triune essence of God and the hypostatic nature of Jesus Christ tell us that diversity operating in unity is a profound mystery and never a formula. Ask a husband and wife that are experiencing heaven on earth through their marriage. Diversity delightfully works itself out as a husband and wife learn to value, appreciate, and celebrate one another's differences. They are clearly different but they are mysteriously and beautifully united as one flesh (Ephesians 6:33). The body of Christ is one body yet it has many parts (I Corinthians 12:12). The whole body was never meant to be a foot or a hand. The body was designed by God to be a conglomeration of different pieces working together as a whole. Do you see the pattern? When God calls for oneness, whether in the Godhead, the deity and humanity of Jesus Christ, the institution of marriage, or the church, He is calling for diversity, and this diversity is usually a beautiful mystery. Unfortunately, when we call for oneness, we have been conditioned to look for sameness.

But on the contrary, Galatians 3:28 is a call to a multifaceted, multidimensional way of life. Let's stop choosing lives that are dreadfully one-dimensional and bland. In my opinion it should be a sin for Christians to make Jesus look boring! The kingdom is like a three-dimensional (3-D) movie, jumping out of heaven's cinema to earth but we don't experience it properly because we don't have the correct lenses on. Our friends, families, churches, ministries, business ventures, literary choices, entertainment, and Christian institutions continue to look and sound like something other than the Diverse Kingdom that God wants us to know, model, and replicate now. The world is far more diversified than the church is and that is a sad fact. Take this in the right context: our churches should look like the world. If the church is active building the kingdom and not just building buildings, our parishes should reflect the Jerusalem we reside in (Acts 1:8). The areas of sports, money, entertainment, music, pain, and technology seem to bring the world together more effectively and genuinely than Jesus appears able to do with His body called the church. Churches keep choosing convenience over kingdom, and as a result, our Christian lives miss their intended fullness. We have little diversity but a lot of excuses for why we remain segregated. There is a danger for us and especially our children when we continue to live for comfort and familiarity and not for the kingdom.

AL AND ERA

When our church started in September of 1995, God determined in its DNA that it would be multi-ethnic, multicultural, and multi-economic. We started meeting for worship back then in the aerobics room of the Franklin YMCA. Our 30 member core had some wonderful times learning together and cutting that new path of kingdom diversity. God was faithful to send some very choice people our way. Some of these people stayed for months, some stayed for years, and some are still with us to this day. If we needed musicians God would send them, and not just any kind of musicians. God sent world class, Grammy nominated musicians and singers to help us in the day of small beginnings! If we needed children's workers God sent them, too. I was twenty-seven years old when we launched and God knew we needed wisdom so He sent a gray haired coupled named Al and Era Jaynes.

Prior to coming to STBC, Al and Era didn't have any in depth, ongoing relationships with black people. Al was sixty-three years old and Era was sixty-four. They had long attended Belmont Church in Nashville where Al served as an elder for over twenty years. As was their custom since 1980, Al and Era would slip away every year and go to a "chandelier swinging" conference in Black Mountain, North Carolina. It was November 24, 1995 and Promise Keepers front man Wellington Boone was scheduled to speak at the conference but was unable to attend so his protégé spoke in his place. In this sea of 3,000 white faces, Garland Hunt, an African American, stood up and challenged the believers in attendance to make some serious social changes. He mentioned how Louis Farrakhan had just attempted to lead one million black men to Washington, DC for what was called "A Day of Atonement". Garland talked about how many black men in America had been caught up with that false movement and how Christianity seemed irrelevant to their cause. He said that black and white relations weren't working in America because it wasn't working in the church. During prayer after the message, God spoke to Al's heart and told him that he needed to leave his all white church and begin attending a church led by an African American man.

When Al and Era left the conference center and went back to their rooms, he told Era that the Lord had spoken to him after Garland Hunt's message. Era asked, "What did the Lord say?" Reluctantly, Al wrote the message down on a pad and handed it to Era. When she read it, she screamed and threw the pad up in the air. Al prepared himself for rejection, but Era said to him, "The Lord said the same thing to me, too!" That next Sunday they pulled up to the YMCA to worship at Strong Tower. On the way in from the parking lot Era looked at Al and said, "If the pastor doesn't preach Jesus we're not staying." They came in, took a seat, and looked around at the diverse group of which they were clearly the oldest people present. That morning I got up to give my pastoral remarks and the first thing that came out of my mouth was, "If I don't preach Jesus, don't come to this church." Al and Era knew they had found their home church and we were blessed to begin living in community with them.

If our Christian experience with God is limited to people who look like us, talk like us, live like us, and believe every theological tenet like us, we will subconsciously and foolishly believe that God Himself is like us and maybe even only for us. We'll think that God is a man or a woman, an American or an African, a Baptist or a Pentecostal, a black person or a white person, a conservative or a liberal, and so on. Jesus expects for us to be in relation with people who are not like us. The tax collectors and sinners were known for loving and greeting people that were just like themselves (Matthew 5:46-47, Luke 6:32), but Jesus expects more from His disciples. He wants us to love our enemies and those opposed to us (Luke 6:35). Jesus wants His people to be drawn to the last, the lost, and the least among us. When our Christian worldview and life experiences stay lopsided and one-sided we unwittingly pull God down to our level and re-create Him after our image (Romans 1:22-23) when in essence we were created in God's image (Genesis 1:27).

This is why God is compelling us to rise upward to be like Him and his Son, to embrace what He embraces. Christians are to be intelligent representatives and intentional reproducers of His Diverse Kingdom on earth until His Son Jesus Christ returns to establish His Diverse Kingdom once and for all. This is the kingdom we will one day enter with billions of people from all walks of life. The rich are a part of this kingdom. The poor are a part of this kingdom. Those struggling with addictions, strong holds, and besetting sins are a part of this kingdom. Our common bond is the only Savior and wise God—Jesus Christ (Acts 2:44, Jude 25). Americans, Africans, Arabs, Native Americans, Asians, Australians, and Europeans are a part of this Diverse Kingdom. Democrats, Republicans, Moderates, and Independents are a part of this Diverse Kingdom. Men, women, and children are a part of God's Diverse Kingdom. Baptists, Pentecostals, and Methodists are a part of this kingdom, and if not already, don't you want to be a part of God's Diverse Kingdom both now and forevermore? Jesus is the King of this kingdom and all you must do is turn from living life your way and place your trust in Him to save you from your sins (Acts 16:30-31). Your life will never be the same, especially as you keep on following Jesus into the realm of God's Diverse Kingdom.

GOD'S DIVERSE KINGDOM COME THROUGH **RACE**

"There is neither Jew nor Greek…" Galatians 3:28a

1. HIS FIRST SERMON WAS ALMOST HIS LAST

What would make a crowd try to kill you after your initial sermon in your hometown? What would turn a delightful congregation into an angry mob? Just bring up the topic of race and watch how quickly the audience turns on you.

Jesus' earthly ministry had just begun somewhere around the age of thirty (Luke 3:23). He was baptized by John the Baptist in the Jordan and was publicly confirmed by His Father and anointed by the Holy Spirit (Luke 3:22). The Spirit then led Jesus into the wilderness where for forty days He fasted and did spiritual battle with Satan (Luke 4:1-13). Jesus successfully withstood Satan's temptations and He came back to Galilee to begin sharing the Word of God with the people. He was received so well that the people glorified Him (Luke 4:15). What a way to start your ministry.

But things would change drastically when Jesus went to Nazareth, a town of possibly 700 people. It was the place where He had been raised since being a young Child. Luke 4:16 reveals that Jesus' custom was to go into the synagogue and read the Scripture. Growing up in Nazareth, the people knew Jesus and His family very well. They knew His father's occupation, His brothers by name, and also His sisters (Mark 6:3). It must have been a common thing to see Jesus participating in worship in the synagogue, but little did the assembled worshippers know they were going to get a bombshell dropped on them that particular day. Of all the scrolls to choose from, the sovereign God chose Isaiah as the Old Testament scripture that would be read that day, and it just so happened by providence that it was Jesus' turn to do the reading. The men in the community would rotate reading the Word of God and on this very day at this very hour it was Jesus' time to make His messianic declaration.

Jesus read the portion of Isaiah that was a well-known prophecy detailing the ministry of the coming Messiah's first advent (Isaiah 61:1-2a). Isaiah wrote His prophecy over eight hundred years prior to this event in the synagogue. Jesus stood up and read the familiar passage about the Anointed One, that is the Christ, and said, *"Today this Scripture is fulfilled in your hearing"* (Luke 4:21). He then closed the book and handed it back to the attendant and sat down. You could probably hear a pin drop after that statement. Jesus made the claim that He was Israel's long awaited Messiah, King, and Deliverer. If you had been there, you probably would have responded the way these people did. The crowd was astounded and stupefied because they did not believe that Jesus could be the Messiah. The Jews felt that Jesus was too normal and familiar of a figure to be the highly anticipated deliverer of the Jewish people. The people rejected Jesus on face value (John 1:11) and judged Him according to the flesh or in mere physical terms (II Corinthians 5:16). He was just too ordinary to be their Messiah (Isaiah 53:2).

Their response led Jesus to say, *"Assuredly, I say to you, no prophet is accepted in His own country"* (Luke 4:24). The people of Jesus' hometown felt that His claim was bogus. No doubt they chalked His claim up to lunacy or demonic possession like the Pharisees would eventually do (John 8:48) because this was not a topic the Jews made light of. They were tired of being oppressed as a nation and they were looking with great anticipation for the emancipator to come from God and set them free. But it was just not the people in Nazareth that rejected Jesus. The majority of the Jews in the South did not receive Jesus as the Messiah either (John 1:11).

ELIJAH, ELISHA, AND GENTILES

Sensing His audience's disdain, Jesus builds on they're attitude of rejection by reminding them of Israel's history. Jesus brings up how Elijah the prophet was rejected by his own people and this caused him to go a Gentile nation to bless a Gentile widow during the days of intense famine in Israel (I Kings 17:8-24). Of all the Jewish widows God could have sent the prophet to, God chose instead to send Elijah to a Gentile. Jesus was making the point that Israel missed the blessing because of they're unbelief, but God still had a witness who trusted Him in a Gentile city called Zarephath. This "filthy" woman benefitted from the grace of God whereas the Jews missed the blessing because of unbelief. Jesus' application of the story of Elijah and the widow stung the people listening that day because it involved God blessing another race of people and not the Jews. Jesus was making the point that since His own people rejected Him then the Gentiles would gladly receive Him and be the beneficiaries of His power and grace. Paul experienced this phenomenon in his ministry with Jews and Gentiles as well (Acts 13:44-52). The Gentiles are the other sheep Jesus talked about in John 10:16, and they are the ones that Jesus will hand the kingdom over to in order to produce its fruit since the Jews by and large rejected their Messiah (Matthew 21:43).

Jesus didn't stop with His point with the Gentile widow. He went on to bring up the Old Testament story of the prophet Elisha healing Naaman the Syrian of his leprosy (II Kings 5:1-19). Jesus makes the same point and that is, there were many lepers in Israel at that time but they didn't get healed. God chose to heal a foreigner because the people of God had turned from Him and turned to idols. God had turned His favor from the Jews to the Gentiles and apparently He would do it again in the face of Israel's rejection of Jesus as the Messiah.

These people first thought Jesus' words were gracious (Luke 4:22), but now they felt He made incendiary comments. The topic of race relations so riled them up that they wanted to kill Him. The Bible says, *"So all those in the synagogue, when they heard these things, were filled with wrath, and rose up and thrust Him out of the city; and they led Him to the brow of the hill on which their city was built, that they might throw Him down over the cliff"* (Luke 4:28-29). Everyone turned on Jesus and wanted to kill Him, but not because He claimed to be the Messiah. The Jews wanted to kill Jesus because they felt He slighted their people and promoted foreigners over them. Jesus, using the topic of race, struck a nerve in the Jews that day.

ARE WE SUPPRESSING OR ADDRESSING?

There are topics that don't always strike the nerves of churchgoers, but I believe the subject of race is one of those topics that rouse the people every time. Either people don't want to hear it and they tune out the speaker, or they listen with an ear to find fault and not an ear to learn. Race, like no other topic in the church, can get the preacher thrown out of the pulpit because race is so explosive, subjective, painful, personal, and convicting. When a black person addresses a white audience on race, the audience usually gets defensive and is visibly irritated. Believe me. I know firsthand. When a black person challenges a black audience to take moral and familial responsibility and stop blaming "the white man", the audience turns on him. Believe me, I know firsthand on this one, too.

When a white person addresses a black audience on the issue of race, the listeners purse their lips and cross their arms signifying their lack of receptivity.

5

If a white pastor wishes to kill off his influence in his white congregation, all he has to do is start talking extensively about race and social justice from a biblical, historical, and practical perspective. He will get dozens of emails from people saying, "I never owned slaves", to, "I wish you would get back to preaching the Bible", to, "It's not my fault", or, "What does this have to do with me?" No wonder so many white pulpits are silent on this issue. White Christians often think if they just ignore it that it will go away. That's the ostrich approach to racial issues. They believe if they bury their heads in the sand and not see the problem then maybe the problem won't see them. The ostrich thinks even though its rear end is foolishly sticking up above ground and its head is fearfully nestled in a hole, maybe the predator will go away. It goes away until the next racial powder keg or hate crime detonates in society. Believers in Jesus often spend more time and energy suppressing the issues than addressing them head on and in a timely manner. I know Peter denied the Lord three times, but we don't need to deny anymore that racism exists in our communities, families, churches, schools, local and federal government, and our world. Racism exists around us because prejudice, judging, and malice still live in each and every one of us. The heart, though regenerated for Christians, is still grossly contaminated. Jesus said so (Matthew 15:18-19, John 2:25). Self–righteousness will cause us to deny and suppress this malady. There can only be healing after we admit that we are sick. Then, and only then, will we begin to experience a change in ourselves that will lead to a change in the world. When we confess that we are blind and cannot see, Jesus us gives us sight and new eyes to see with.

The world doesn't look to Christians for answers in this area because we don't have any unfortunately. The answers are there in the gospel, but because we don't live, believe or apply these answers our Christian experience is irrelevant, devoid, and uninspiring. We've lost our saltiness. We are years behind mainstream society in regards to racial progress and ethnic diversity, and that's not saying much when we observe the existence of racism and the subtleties of segregation still thriving and prevalent in our culture. The world is ill equipped to deal adequately with race and Christians are too busy doing spiritual stuff to deal with race. What a tragedy.

PAUL VS. THE LYNCH MOB

The preacher is all right as long as he stays away from preaching on race. If a pastor cares about his approval ratings then he should stay far from preaching on racial issues. Paul learned this lesson when he was ministering to the Jews in Jerusalem (Acts 21 and 22). Paul was already a wanted man because of his love for the Gentiles. Jesus put a calling on Paul's life to minister effectively among the Gentiles (Acts 9:15). In this particular episode in Acts 21 the people grabbed Paul while he was in the temple because they assumed he brought a Gentile named Trophimus into the temple, which was forbidden (Acts 21:29). After grabbing Paul, they commenced to beating on him. He would have been beaten to a pulp if the Roman soldiers had not broken through the mob and rescued Paul from their clutches (Acts 21:30-32).

Once he was led to the barracks, Paul asked the Roman commander in the Greek language if he could speak to the people (Acts 21:37). The commander gave Paul permission to speak and he did so in the Hebrew language, and this made the people become silent (Acts 22:2). They wanted to hear what he had to say, so Paul took the opportunity to share his testimony. The crowd listened to him until he brought up the topic of race. In Acts 22:21-22 the Bible says, *"Then He said to me, 'Depart, for I will send you far from here to the Gentiles.' And they listened to him until this word, and they raised their voices and said, 'Away with such a fellow from the earth, for he is not fit to live!'"*

Did Paul, like Jesus, mention the Gentiles on purpose in order to get to the true heart of the people? Who knows, but I believe that race reveals our true hearts, our fears, and intentions when the necessary button is pushed. Jesus said that money is an indicator of where our hearts are before God (Matthew 6:21) and I believe race is also a prime indicator of where we stand relationally and spiritually (I John 3:14, 4:20-21). If racial gunpowder and ethnic explosives are stored in our hearts then the right word or incident will light our fuses and we will explode. Because of the fallen nature of man and the darkness and depravity of our hearts we all have some racial explosives in our hearts, but the question is, how much? Has the Holy Spirit begun to remove the dynamite stick by stick, or are we in denial that these weapons of mass destruction actually exist within us (Jeremiah 17:9)?

EXAMINE YOURSELF

It would be easy to gang up on the Jews of old and wag a self-righteous finger in their faces, and not point thumbs at us. We need to use these biblical references to ask ourselves the tough questions. Do I get ticked off whenever race is mentioned? Do I judge people on appearances and make personal assumptions about them based on race without knowing them? Do I shut down and close up when the topic of race is preached or written about? Do I immediately judge black speakers as blaming white people and white speakers as being insincere and apathetic? Do I get upset if someone suggests that I should apologize for the sins of my ancestors? Do I get weary of news programs and documentaries that focus on the state of race relations in America? Do I believe that America doesn't have a race problem? Do I dismiss the truth when spoken by a particular person or people group? Do I suppress animosity towards innocent people solely because they belong to a different ethnicity?

Everyone will get wounded, insulted, and offended working through race matters. There is no "Easy Button" to press and make everything ok or go away. It only becomes manageable and even successful when we journey hand and hand together through past, present, and personal deficiencies saying, "We're going to love each other no matter what." If the love, truth, and grace of God demonstrated through Jesus Christ are not enough for the church to walk this path together towards healing and abundant life, is there any hope for the world?

I am one who believes there is power in our gospel. This power is made manifest when we believe it (Ephesians 1:19). If we consider ourselves to be preachers, pastors, teachers, leaders, and followers of Christ who already died with Christ when He died on Calvary (Romans 6:3, Galatians 2:20, Colossians 3:1-4) what can men do to us? Ask yourself: Will your first sermon, composition, or discussion on race be your last? Hopefully not, but bear in mind that as you walk this path everyone won't walk it with you. You will more than likely get people upset with you for all of the right reasons, but that's a good thing. Welcome to ministry with Jesus Christ and His call to advance, promote, and reflect God's Diverse Kingdom.

2. THE "S" WORD

Prejudice is a learned sin and what makes prejudice contagious is the ability of one people group to call other people derogatory names. Jesus didn't even escape this kind of ignorant categorization when He walked the earth. His own people the Jews said to Him, *"Do we not say rightly that You are a Samaritan and have a demon?"* (John 8:48) That terminology was meant to hurt and belittle Jesus in front of everyone. The Jews wanted to tear Him down so they decided to call Him a name that took on a very strong, negative connotation in that day. To call Jesus a Samaritan, the dreaded "S- word", may be the equivalent of a white person calling a black person the "N-word" today.

HOW IT ALL GOT STARTED

When the nation of Israel split into two kingdoms in 931 BC, the Northern Kingdom and the Southern Kingdom, the ten tribes of the Northern Kingdom resided in what was known as Samaria. King Omri bought land from Shemer, and built a city on it called Samaria (I Kings 16:24). Because there wasn't one godly king in the northern lineage of kings, Samaria came to represent idolatry, godlessness, and gross immorality at its worse. When King Ahab ascended to the throne after his father Omri, he made Samaria the capital of the Northern Kingdom just as Bethlehem was the capital city of the Southern Kingdom. Ahab reigned from Samaria for twenty-two years and he married a Sidonian named Jezebel who brought Baalism to the Jewish people in unprecedented ways.

The Assyrian army defeated the Northern Kingdom of Israel in 722 BC, and many of the Israelites were subsequently carried away by captivity into Assyria (II Kings 17:5-6). The Bible says, *"Then the king of Assyria brought people from Babylon, Cuthah, Ava, Hamath, and from Sepharvaim, and placed them in the cities of Samaria instead of the children of Israel; and they took possession of Samaria and dwelt in its cities."* (II Kings 17:24) When these foreigners occupied Samaria they brought with them their false gods and their deviant behavior. Even though the king of Assyria had a Jewish priest return to the land to *"teach them the rituals of the God of the land"* (17:27), the rituals of the pagan deities won out. The remaining Israelites left in the land intermarried with these pagans and produced a people of mixed racial ancestry and mixed religion.

The Jews in the South would come to know the Samaritans as "dogs", that is, unclean animals. Samaritan women would be considered perpetually unclean by the Jews because they were thought to be on their monthly cycle at all times. This tension would mount over the centuries between the Jews and the Samaritans to the point where the Samaritans built a temple in Gerazim to rival the temple built in Jerusalem. The Samaritans traced their lineage back to Jacob, their father (John 4:12), and not to father Abraham. They only recognized the first five books of the Bible called the Pentateuch, leaving the Jews to consider them as being heretics.

When the Jews of the Southern Kingdom returned home to Judea from their seventy-year captivity to Babylon, their plans to rebuild Jerusalem were temporarily halted by the Samaritans (Ezra 4:1-24). When Nehemiah received permission from Xerxes to rebuild the walls of Jerusalem in 444BC his primary opposition to seeing this project through to completion was from Sanballat and the army of Samaria (Nehemiah 4:1-3). The Samaritans were a thorn in the Jews' side. So by the time you get to Jesus' era, animosity and hatred had been building and brewing for 400 years between the two people groups to the point where they would not come into contact with one another. When a Jew in southern Judea wanted to travel north to Galilee he would not travel the direct route through Samaria. Instead, he would go around Samaria via the Jordan River route so as not to get Samaritan dirt on his sandals.

JESUS, THE RADICAL ONE

Jesus intentionally going through Samaria was a major deal (John 4:4). In his gospel account, John let us know the racial climate of the day by reminding us that Jews and Samaritans have no dealings (John 4:9). Nevertheless, Jesus the Radical One chose to go through Samaria much to the chagrin of His disciples. Jesus not only went through Samaria, but He also stopped there and had a conversation with an "unclean" Samaritan woman in broad daylight. The Bible says that Jesus initiated a conversation with the woman by asking her for something to drink (John 4:7). This took the woman off guard because

Jewish men, yet alone rabbis, did not talk to Samaritans, especially Samaritan women at that.

Side note: If you want things to change you have to be willing to be an agent of change. You have to be radical sometimes. If you wish to follow Jesus for real you have to begin taking the initiative and reaching out to others that you were told were off limits. You have to do different things in order to see things change for the better. Bear in mind that the Jews had the prominence and the power when it came to their relationship with the Samaritans. This means that Jesus represented the oppressor, so no wonder the lady was shocked when Jesus initiated a redemptive kind of contact. In terms of reconciliation between two sides at odds, the historical oppressor bears the responsibility to begin the healing process with the oppressed.

The beauty of this story is also seen in the fact that Jesus never stopped being whom He was in order to reach this woman. In other words, He never stopped being Jewish to reach a Samaritan because the woman knew He was a Jew. She may have known Jesus was Jewish by His accent, how He wore His hair, the manner of clothing He wore, or His mannerisms. In the call to Kingdom Diversity, never stop being the person you are in order to reach others evangelistically. Be sensitive to various cultures and learn from them, but never stop being the person God made you to be. Become all things to all men while remaining true to who you are (I Corinthians 9:22). A white man raised in the suburbs shouldn't try to speak street slang, listen to hip-hop, and sag in his attire in order to reach young African Americans in the inner city. He will make Jesus and himself look bad!

TRADING SPIT

Jesus was willing to drink from this Samaritan woman's cup. He was willing to trade saliva with a woman who had a live in boyfriend and five former husbands. Jesus would soon carry her sin on the cross so I suppose carrying her saliva would be another demonstration of His love for this "dog". She received His offer of living water because she knew that He legitimately cared for her. Jesus was probably the first man, Jew or Samaritan, who showed her real love with no strings attached.

The love of God broke down the racial barriers that afternoon. When the woman left and the twelve disciples returned, Jesus invited them to join Him in sharing the gospel of the kingdom with the Samaritans (John 4:39-42). As I see the text in John 4, it doesn't appear that the disciples joined Jesus on this particular weekend mission's trip. There is no mention that the Twelve took

Him up on his offer and stayed with Him. Jesus appears to have walked this road alone, at least for now.

SAMARITAN SUCCESS STORIES

What a shame. The disciples missed a golden opportunity. They were not ready to follow Jesus across the railroad tracks and over that ethnic bridge just yet. They weren't ready to mix it up with those mixed up Samaritans. The disciples couldn't escape the Samaritans because Jesus kept them before the disciples in His sermons and intentionally included them in His ministry. There was the time that Jesus healed ten lepers and at least one of them was a Samaritan (Luke 17:11-19). Isn't that beautiful? A crippling disease brought Jews and Samaritans together. "Healthy" Jews and Samaritans won't come together but sick ones will. I am convinced that when people have something in common with one another, even if it's sickness, they will form a bond that cannot be easily broken. Community comes when we acknowledge our common unity, and in this case leprosy unified the lepers across racial lines.

A Jewish Savior healed a Samaritan leper and he was the only one out of ten to come back and thank Jesus (Luke 17:15-19)! I wonder if that once integrated community of outcasts returned back to segregated lives once they got well? I hope Jesus was able to rally these men together just as much as the leprosy did but we'll never know. What we need to do is bring this story up to our time and ask is Jesus able to bring men and women together more than our pain ever could? I have seen different kinds of people rally together in times of crisis but not always in times of peace. If people would admit their sin sickness regardless of their ethnicity and depend on a Jewish Savior that loves all people and desires to heal them, we might begin to see things change in our churches. If things change in our churches then things will change for the better in culture.

We can't forget how Jesus used a Samaritan as the hero of His parable about being a good neighbor in Luke 10:25-37. It's amazing how we can love this story but miss the racial ramifications Jesus made in it. The Jewish man Jesus shared the parable with couldn't even say it was the Samaritan who ended up being the neighbor to the Jewish man who had fallen among thieves. The lawyer could only say, "He" who showed mercy was the man's true neighbor. The lawyer couldn't dignify the Samaritan by acknowledging his ethnicity because in his mind and upbringing, there was nothing good about a Samaritan. Jesus then told that Jewish man and all those listening to go and follow the Samaritan man's example. That was a profound point and it probably offended many of the Jews.

There was also the time when gentle John the apostle whom Jesus loved and James his brother wanted to burn down a Samaritan village for rejecting Jesus' request to stay there before going to Jerusalem (Luke 9:51-56). This encounter happens near the end of Jesus' ministry so this means that when the Jews had finally warmed up to the idea of going through Samaria and staying with "those people", the Samaritans had changed in their acceptance of Jesus. They would not accept Him since He was going to Jerusalem to be with "those people" the Jews.

James and John's true feelings surfaced and they asked Jesus for permission to call down fire from God and consume those despicable dogs the way Elijah did with the prophets of Baal in I Kings 18. Wait a minute. James and John assumed that God was prejudiced like they were. They figured that God felt the same way about the Samaritans as they did. They ascribed to God their hatred and lack of tolerance for the Samaritans. Isn't that how we think unfortunately? Our prejudice may not be as overt but it is at times covert and we think that God signs off on it. James and John thought God would answer that horrible prayer. Secondly, they also got the Bible story about Elijah wrong. Elijah called down fire on the animal sacrifice on the altar and not upon the prophets of Baal (I Kings 18:38). Yes, Elijah killed the four hundred prophets of Baal that day with the sword (18:40), but that was for the purpose of cleansing the land of the leaven of false religion. That was not a racial hate crime in Elijah's day. This exemplifies how we can take Scripture out of context to support our selfish, sinful, and prejudice ways. I remember hearing people who did not believe in interracial dating and marriage misuse and misquote the Bible as a way to support their prejudice. That's no surprise because the Bible was also used to support the brutality of the Crusades, the Spanish Inquisition, the African Slave Trade, the Holocaust, and mass Indian relocations to reservations.

SAMARITAN LOVER

As far as Jesus was concerned being called a Samaritan was probably a compliment to the multi-cultural life He lived. Jesus was indeed a Samaritan lover so being called the "S-word" was received as a blessing even though it was given as a curse. No wonder He could say in the Sermon on the Mount, *"Blessed are you when they revile and persecute you, and say all kinds of evil against you falsely for my sake. Rejoice and be exceedingly glad, for great is your reward in heaven, for so they persecuted the prophets who were before you."* (Matthew 5:11-12) Jesus lived what He preached and He never returned evil for evil or ignorance for ignorance (I Peter 2:21-23).

In my years as a pastor I have been called the "N-word" by whites that I had done my best to minister to. I have grown to take their intended insults as compliments. Blacks have ridiculed me for having white people in our church, and implied I wasn't a "real brother." I have grown to take their intended insults as compliments. I have been told that some of my white parishioners get called "N- lovers" because they go to a multi-ethnic church with an African American pastor or because they adopt children of color. The good news is that they see it as a blessed, badge of honor.

Jesus kept on passing through Samaria in His travels. He included the region of Samaria in His commission to the Jews found in Acts 1:8 which says, *"But you shall receive power when the Holy Spirit has come upon you; and you shall be witnesses of Me in Jerusalem, and in all Judea and Samaria, and to the end of the earth."* When the gospel finally reached Samaria in Acts 8:4-25 through the efforts of Philip, the church in Jerusalem sent Peter and John, those reputed to be pillars (Galatians 2:9) to come and pray for them that they might receive the Holy Spirit. Peter and John had to *"lay their hands on them"* (Acts 8:17) in order for the Samaritans to receive the Holy Spirit. There is a lesson to be learned in that gesture of obedience. God would only show up once there was some physical touching and agreeing going on between two people groups. One man had to touch another man for the Spirit of God to flow. David the psalmist said, *"Behold, how good and how pleasant it is for brethren to dwell together in unity! It is like the precious oil upon the head, running down on the beard, the beard of Aaron…"* (Psalm 133:1-2).

Moses anointed Aaron (Exodus 29:7). The brother raised in privilege anointed the brother raised in slavery. It is no wonder the anointing oil is symbolic of the Holy Spirit! I am a witness that the Holy Spirit shows up and begins to anoint and drench His people with His love, joy, and peace whenever we touch one another in agreement. This kind of anointing breaks the yoke of bondage (Isaiah 10:27). The anointing of God is manifested whenever God's people touch one another, lay hands on one another, lift one another's burdens, and choose to dwell together in unity. We love Jesus because we can "touch" Him with the feelings of our infirmities (Hebrews 4:15, KJV), and since Jesus is touched by our touch, He can sympathize with us in our struggles. What we lack in the race issue today is sympathy. We lack sympathy because we lack touch with one another, but Jesus always dwells in the midst of His church whenever His people come together in prayer, touch each other, hold hands, and stand together in agreement in Jesus' name (Matthew 18:19-20, KJV).

HARVEST TIME!

The one and only Holy Spirit would baptize the Samaritans into the body of Christ with their Jewish brothers and sisters, making them one (I Corinthians 12:13). The two disciples who once despised going through that neighborhood of half-breeds with Jesus, were now going through that area preaching the gospel of the kingdom in the name of Jesus (Acts 8:25). Only God can change hearts that way, and the proof that your heart has changed is that your feet change. Your feet follow your heart and your heart follows Jesus, and He was intentional to go to those people and we should be, also.

God placed Samaria in the middle of the Jews' world and there was no getting around it. God will place "those people" right in the center of your world and you won't be able to get around them. They may live in your neighborhood, work on your job, marry into the family, or sit down next to you at church. Whatever the scenario, don't you think it is time to finally go through Samaria and sit down? Jesus said in John 4:35, *"Do you not say, 'There are still four months and then comes the harvest'? Behold, I say to you, lift up your eyes and look at the fields, for they are already white for harvest!'"*

The harvest for the Diverse Kingdom is ripe but the reconcilers are few. Don't you think it's time to share some conversation with "that person"? Don't you think it's time to have coffee with "that guy" or "that gal" from Samaria? But please beware. You may get called some names and you may not get invited to some functions, but the good news is that you and Jesus will have that in common! We say we want to be more like Jesus, but are we really ready for that? If you are ready, watch out. A revival might break out, and if it does, it will change your entire life from the inside out!

3. IS BLACK BEAUTIFUL?

I grew up in Baltimore, Maryland going to a Baptist church that was 100% African American in membership. I thought the word "Baptist" was a synonym for "black" because the only Baptists I knew were black folks. My grandfather, the Rev. Hezekiah Williamson, Sr. was the pastor. He and my father, Harold Williamson, Sr. built the church by laying the cement and placing the bricks. Like most churches in that era there was a painting of Jesus and John the Baptist right behind the pulpit over the hidden baptism pool. As a child I thought the painting didn't fit with our church because the images of Jesus and John were that of white men. Even in the hallway and in my grandfather's office there were pictures of a blonde haired, blue-eyed Jesus. I hardly ever saw white people in my neighborhood and the only time I saw them in our church was in those pictures.

And speaking of pictures, I loved the Renaissance art period in junior high school because the paintings of Leonardo De Vinci and Michelangelo resembled comic book characters. They painted their figures with definition and muscle tone and I liked that. I could draw a little myself and I could identify with their works a little more than with Van Gogh and other abstract artists. But what was painfully obvious to me was how all of the Bible characters and even the angels during this period of rebirth were represented as Caucasian men and women. When I opened up our huge family Bible on the coffee table there would yet again be caricatures of white people drawn and painted as prominent Bible characters. Adam was white. Moses was white. David was white, and of course Jesus was white.

When I went to college I began to hear about the infamous "Curse of Ham" doctrine taught from Genesis 9:25-27. I also began to hear rumblings that the mark that God put on Cain for killing his brother Abel was black skin (Genesis 4:15). My professors didn't teach me these things per se but I heard about them through the grapevine. My curiosity was aroused and a passion to learn how God's Word was twisted in the past and what He truly had to say on the subjects of race and black people began to stir me.

READ BLACK MAN READ!

I began to see how the game was played: Black people were said to be in the pages of the Bible but it was only when it came to a curse. However, people of color weren't in the Bible when it came to making positive contributions. Sociology impacted theology and theology reinforced sociology. It was circular reasoning at its best. God impressed upon my heart to search out other secondary sources of Biblical knowledge. When I graduated from seminary in 1992, I began to read books written by black theologians that shed new light on the presence and positive contributions of Black people in the Bible. These sources may have been lesser known but they were still sound. Black authors like Rev. Dwight McKissic, Carl Ellis, Dr. Tony Evans, and Joel C. Freeman began opening up my mind like never before.

It has been said, "If you want to hide something from a black man, put it in a book." That stereotype didn't work with me. A whole new world opened up to me as I turned each page. McKissic's little book, <u>Beyond Roots: In Search of Blacks in the Bible</u>, and his more scholarly follow up with Dr. Evans, <u>Beyond Roots 2: A Deeper Look at Blacks in the Bible</u>, changed my life. While reading these works I would sometimes laugh and say to myself, "Now, why haven't I heard this stuff before?" The information has always been there, it was just not important enough for my white professors to share with me. I learned great theology from them but I had to learn about myself on my own and from my own.

In order to get hyped up before a big boxing match, the great boxer Muhammad Ali used to shout face to face with his friend and corner man Drew "Bundini" Brown. They would say, "Rumble, young man rumble!" Well, knowing the fight that I was in as a black man on a quest for God's wisdom and knowledge I used to encourage myself by saying, "Read, black man read!" As I turned the pages and absorbed the data, my appreciation for God and my self-confidence began to grow. For the first time while reading the Bible I saw for myself that God used, blessed, and honored my African ancestors. A fire was aroused in my soul, but as you could imagine, that fire was soon challenged with the chilly waters of sarcasm. When I shared my discoveries with my white brothers, many of them wrote me off and dismissed my findings on face value, or should I say "Black face value."

I discovered quickly that if a notable white author or a highly visible white minister didn't subscribe to the materials I read or the comments I espoused then my information was considered skeptical by the majority. In other words, my words were not valid until a white minister validated them. This comes from the fact that white people in America have been conditioned to not personally trust me initially or the words that come out of my mouth. Michael Emerson, author of the groundbreaking book <u>Divided By Faith</u> calls our racially divided and preconditioned culture a "racialized society". Dr. Emerson writes, "In the post-Civil Rights United States, the racialized society is one in which intermarriage rates are low, residential separation and socioeconomic inequality are the norm, our definitions of personal identity and our choices of intimate associations reveal racial distinctiveness, and where 'we are never unaware of the race of a person with whom we interact.'" (p. 7) It's been my experience that people like to be with people who are like themselves. We have strong opinions about other people groups, so much so that these perceptions have been engrained into our thinking, everyday choices, and way of life. This engraining shows up in where we choose to live, go to school, go to church, and whom we marry. Society enforced the notion that blacks were to be known primarily for their brawn and not for their brains, and any "N-word" that aspired towards learning had to be put in his or her place.

Needless to say, my concordances, Bible dictionaries and commentaries were all of a sudden questionable. The truth of the matter is that they were the same sources that my white colleagues and professors used and taught me to use. My personal library looked like their libraries but our conclusions were somehow vastly different. I remember preaching in all white settings in the early 90's on the topic of racial reconciliation. Racial Reconciliation was the catchphrase back then. It was the term of choice for progressive believers who were serious about "knocking down the walls" of racial division. I and other black ministers received quite a few invitations to speak at all white churches and colleges during this period. I rarely heard white ministers speak on the matter of racial reconciliation. I guess they didn't feel they had much to say or contribute on this topic. They may have felt they had no real authority or true reference point to speak on it because they lacked viable relationships and experiences. I also know some were playing it safe and chose to be silent and that silence amazed and frustrated me. I felt these guys were more concerned about being white than about being right. To add injury to insult, whenever I spoke and would mention my new findings about the black presence in the Bible and God's plan for blacks, I would get immediate resistance. I had what Edward Gilbreath wrote about in his book, <u>Reconciliation Blues:</u>

A Black Evangelical's Inside View of White Christianity. Gilbreath said, "The loneliness of being 'the only black,' the frustration of being expected to represent your race but being stifled when you try. The hidden pain of being invited to the table but shut out from meaningful decisions about the table's future. These 'reconciliation blues' are about the despair of knowing it's still business as usual, even in the friendly context of Christian fellowship and ministry." (p.19)

I would share how God created all of us from the blood of one man, Adam (Acts 17:26), and how He has redeemed us from the blood of one Lamb, Jesus Christ, the last Adam (Revelation 5:9, I Corinthians 15:45). I would make clear how God carried on His plan of repopulating the earth through Noah's three sons Shem, Ham, and Japheth after the flood (Genesis 9:18-19). That God specifically established where they would live and how they would seek Him and find Him through His Son Jesus Christ (Acts 17:26-31). I explained how Shem's name meant "olive" or "dusky" and that he was the progenitor of the Semitic and even Arabic peoples through an un-ordained encounter that Abraham had with an Egyptian woman named Hagar (Genesis 16:1-15). I taught them that Ham's name means "black" or "dark" and that he was the father of all dark skinned peoples and Mongoloids. I mentioned how Japheth's name in the Hebrew means "bright" or "fair" and that he was the ancestral father of the Caucasian people groups. God made it where Noah's three sons ranged in complexion and He decided to repopulate the entire earth through them.

Once I preached and the services were over, without fail white people would rush up to me protesting my comments before my foot even hit the ground from the platform. I realized that this information was just as new for them as it was for me. They thought that my conclusions were absurd. They said that I should leave that race stuff alone and just preach the gospel. I would reply, "This is the gospel. It's the whole counsel of God I am proclaiming (Acts 20:27)." Bear in mind that since the inception of this nation Black people had to accept everything presented to them about God from the white man. Black people didn't have the voice, the power, the respect, or in some cases, the understanding to speak up and disagree with the white power base (Proverbs 18:17). Blacks could not question authority, and when it came to religion, everything positive was white, including Jesus, and everything negative was black, including Ham and his cursed descendents the Canaanites.

In those formative days of our nation, black people didn't write theology books or own printing presses. Their art wasn't displayed in museums. The white perspective was the "right perspective" and the only perspective for that matter. Biblical truth was seen through white eyes and white lenses only for over 400 years. Some of the lies that the institution of slavery instilled in the American people were that Black people were lazy, ignorant, and not to be trusted. Blacks were conceptualized as sexually deviant cannibals who had their lustful eyes set on the white woman. The white church reinforced these lies by saying that Ham had a homosexual encounter with his father Noah and was cursed as a result. However, a nonbiased reading of the text in Genesis 9:21-27 will reveal that Canaan was cursed and not Ham. Even still, the damage had been done. The dreaded "Curse of Ham" doctrine was drilled into America's religious and democratic fabrics. Once again, Ham and his descendents were black when it came to a curse of servitude but Ham and his descendents were not black when it came to positive contributions for the scope of Christianity. For instance, Simon of Cyrene always seems to strangely "whiten up" on film adaptations of the crucifixion. The same is true in most commentaries. The Bible Knowledge Commentary: New Testament Edition that I love and use says on page 88, "Simon of Cyrene, a city in North Africa populated with many Jews, was forced to carry the cross…" We know that Jews lived in Africa, but we can't forget that Africans lived there, too. Then there's The Liberty Commentary of the New Testament that says, "Cyrene was a district in North Africa where many Jews lived. They had a synagogue in Jerusalem (Acts 6:9), so numbers of them must have been constant there" (p. 88). The New Illustrated Bible Commentary states, "Cyrene, located in North Africa was home to a large number of Jews" (p. 1199). The NIV Study Bible, 1985 edition records, "*Cyrene*: An important city in Libya in North Africa that had a large Jewish population. *Simon*: Probably a Jew who was in Jerusalem to celebrate the Passover..." (p. 1528). These comments all suggest that Simon was more than likely Jewish and not African or black. The writers just couldn't bring themselves to say that a man from a city in Africa may have actually been a black African. Why can't the man who carried Christ's cross be a black man? I'll tell you why. Simon can't be a black man because he makes a positive contribution to the scope of Christianity, that's why. This is a subtle form of evangelical discrimination.

Sociology and Hollywood have tragically skewed and affected our theology and hermeneutics, but as for me, I strongly believe and proudly teach that Simon was a black African. He was picked out of the crowd of Jews and Romans because of the fact that his black skin stood out. A black man bore the cross for Christ so that Christ could bear the sins of the world on the cross (I Peter 2:24). Descendents of the three sons of Noah were present that Good Friday in the form of the Romans, Jews, and Simon from North Africa. O' how we need more black men to carry the cross of Jesus today! Hearing of a black Simon may not mean much to my white family members but it may keep some of my ebony brothers from carrying other things that are deadly to themselves and society. If Simon is a black man I can all the more encourage black men to carry their crosses for Jesus. Simon's sons Alexander and Rufus (Mark 15:21) must have been terrified by their dad's public involvement with a bludgeoned Christ that dreadful day in the face of an angry mob. Seeing their father so closely associated with this Man Jesus would forever change their lives. Their names are mentioned in the gospel account of Mark with such familiarity that they must have gone on to be standouts in the body of Christ (Romans 16:13). You see, when I preach this passage I instill hope to generations, especially to those of my own ethnicity. What black boy today doesn't need to see his black father publicly identify with Jesus? And by the way, that's not the image of the black family we'll see on the news this evening.

Africans were considered pagan idolaters in need of "evangelization" because the Europeans said their primitive religions were barbaric, satanic, and demoralizing. Over time the majority of whites in our nation developed these negative perceptions of blacks, and some blacks even developed these mindsets toward themselves and other blacks. When you hear a lie long enough you begin to believe it is the truth. Black hatred from whites turned into self-hatred by blacks and many of us are still dealing with these poisonous perceptions to this day. Black life is not seen as precious life worth preserving. Entrenched myths don't die easily.

When I began to read the Bible with new lenses I soon realized that Jesus spent time in Africa as a child (Matthew 2:13-15). My soul leapt within me when I saw this once I graduated from seminary! Growing up I had heard of "Shaft in Africa" but not "Jesus in Africa". The Bible states that Jesus and His parents went to Egypt to flee from Herod's lethal attack. This led Matthew to quote the prophet Hosea, *"Out of Egypt I have called my Son"* (Hosea 11:1). At this point I have to state the obvious and say that Egypt is a country on the continent of Africa. Egypt is not in Europe. Not many people notice this fact because of how the media has conditioned us in the past. Hollywood didn't believe the Egyptians were Africans in the golden days of Elizabeth Taylor and Charlton Heston. The Egyptians, with their advancements in medicine, writing, architecture, and science were too smart to be black. They had to have been white Europeans, right? Wrong! The Egyptians were Africans.

I kept on reading the Bible and saw that Christianity reached the continent of Africa long before Europeans on slave ships ever did. In Acts 8, which occurred in the first half of the first century, Philip led the Ethiopian Eunuch to saving faith in Jesus, baptized him, and sent him home rejoicing (Acts 8:26-39). To this day a church called the Coptic Church resides in Ethiopia and sects of Ethiopian Jews still live in Ethiopia as well as Israel. This means the gospel reached the shores of Africa hundreds of years before slave-trading Europeans arrived in the mid-15th century. The Black Muslims of the Nation of Islam must know that Christianity was not first introduced to Africans when the slave traders arrived in 1444, thus according to them making Christianity "the white man's religion". The truth is, Arabic Muslims enslaved Africans long before Europeans ever did and Africans enslaved Africans before the white man bought into the franchise.

According to Young's Analytical Concordance of the Bible, Noah's middle son Ham, as we said before, name means, "dark colored". (p. 443) Ham had four sons named Mizraim, Cush, Put, and Canaan (Genesis 10:6). "Mizraim" is the ancestral father of the Egyptians, and "Cush" is the progenitor of the Ethiopians. One famous Cushite was a black man named Nimrod. Nimrod not only built Babel but he also built other cities and was called a mighty one on the earth and a mighty hunter before the Lord (Genesis 10:8-12). The Bible says in Zephaniah 3:10, *"From beyond the rivers of Ethiopia My worshippers. The daughter of My dispersed ones, shall bring My offering. (NKJV)"* Psalm 68:31 says, *"Envoys will come out of Egypt; Ethiopia will quickly stretch out her hands to God."* Some see these passages as prophetic words concerning the ability of Africans and their descendents to worship God with emotion, energy, and exuberance. There may be some truth to that.

I put down my white, western lenses and picked up my new "Diverse Kingdom Lenses" and read the Bible and saw that civilization began somewhere in Africa according to Genesis 2:13. It was within the land of Cush that God established humanity. Wow! This means that Eden was located in what we call Africa and it would not be incorrect to refer to Adam and Eve as Africans—but calm down. Take a deep breath. The sound you just heard was some of our white forefathers rolling over in their graves. I'll comment on Adam and Eve's color later in this chapter.

EBONY AND IVORY

I kept reading the Bible and saw that in addition to Sarah, Abraham married an Egyptian woman named Hagar and together they had a son named Ishmael (Genesis 16:3, 11). Moses married a Cushite woman named Zipporah (Exodus 2:21, Numbers 12:1) that his sister Miriam apparently didn't agree with (Number 12:1-15). Miriam made such a big deal out of Zipporah's skin color that God changed hers for a while! Zipporah was a godly woman who saved Moses' life from God (Exodus 4:24-26). As a type of Christ she saved him by blood and obedience. Zipporah gave Moses two sons named Gershom (Exodus 2:22) and Eliezer (Exodus 18:4).

Do you remember the days when many white, conservative, evangelical, fundamental, Christian colleges and institutions once taught that God's Word didn't encourage or endorse interracial marriage based on a faulty interpretation of Deuteronomy 7:1-4? This mandate was especially true between whites and blacks. The truth is God forbade intermarriage of the Jewish people with other nations based on "religious" practices and not racial heritage. Somehow these teachers and scholars missed how the Jews married Gentile converts to Judaism like when Boaz married Ruth from the country of Moab. His God became her God and His people became her people (Ruth 2:16). Under the New Covenant Paul's admonition for the basis of Christian marriage was found in I Corinthians 7:39. He said the person you intend to marry simply needed to be *"in the Lord"*. The light and dark reference Paul made in the context of being unequally yoked in II Corinthians 6:14 was about spiritual opposites and not racial differences!

It's astounding how quickly evangelical Christians leave the Bible and hide behind cultural challenges when they discuss interracial dating and marriage. I believe some parents would rather their sons and daughters bring home someone of their same race who is spiritually lost rather than someone of another ethnicity that is saved and on fire for Jesus. I remember hearing the old deterrent to interracial marriage, "What about the children that could come from this union? They will be confused about their racial identity." That argument was a poor cover up for prejudice.

BLACKS IN THE BIBLE

The only things black about my Bible were the cover and the letters until I started using my new lenses. I learned about Zipporah's black father and priest Jethro. As a priest this man knew God before he knew Moses. He became one of Moses' chief advisors (Exodus 18:1-27). His black son Hobab became Moses' eyes in the wilderness (Numbers 10:29-32). A Jewish man named Salmon married a Canaanite prostitute named Rahab (Matthew 1:5, Joshua 2:1). Rahab saved the two Jewish spies lives and put a scarlet cord in her window as a sign to save her household from destruction at the hands of Israel as they came to conquer Jericho (Joshua 2:15-21). When I was taught the Old Testament in bible college Rahab the Canaanite wasn't considered a black woman because she did something positive. Through her marriage to a Jewish man she was directly grafted into the ancestral line of the Messiah Jesus (Matthew 1:5). The same was true for another woman of color in Jesus' family tree named Tamar (Matthew 1:2). She was Judah's daughter-in-law and his unsuspecting baby's momma. Judah had a sleazy, one night encounter with Tamar when he roamed the land of Canaan for a season (Genesis 38:1-26). Ruth the Moabite (Ruth 1:4, Matthew 1:5) and Bathsheba (II Samuel 12:24-25, Matthew 1:6) were two more women of color mentioned in Jesus' lineage with direct ties to Ham. Bathsheba was a descendent of Sheba and he was a son of Ham (Genesis 10:7). She was married to a Hittite named Uriah (II Samuel 11:3) and his family tree can also be traced back to Heth, son of Canaan, son of Ham (Genesis 10:15). With exception to Mary, four of the five women mentioned in Jesus' genealogy in Matthew chapter 1 were descendents of Ham, Noah's black son.

With those kinds of genetics in His family, I wouldn't be surprised if Jesus the Israelite had an "afro" hairstyle and dark skin. Hey wait a minute—the book of Revelation describes Jesus as having hair like wool and feet resembling burnished bronze (Revelation 1:14-15, 2:18)! Jesus was probably a dark, Jewish man with no special features that would attract people to Him (Isaiah 53:2). This means if Jesus had blonde hair and blue eyes the way He is often portrayed in our churches and museums He would have definitely drawn a lot of attention to Himself in those days but for the all of the wrong reasons! A blonde haired, blue eyed, white-skinned Jesus would have easily stood out in the garden of Gethsemane the night Jesus was arrested (Matthew 26:47-48) the same way He stood out in my grandfather's church.

But wait, there's more. While in Egypt, the patriarch Joseph married an Egyptian woman named Asenath (Genesis 41:45) and had two sons named Ephraim and Manasseh (Genesis 41:50-52). Jacob blessed Joseph's sons as his own and integrated them into the tribal ancestry of Israel (Genesis 48:1-20). The Bible tells us that an unnamed and apparently expendable Cushite ran with the news to tell King David that his son Absalom had died (II Samuel 18:19-32). A Cushite named Ebed-Melech rescued Jeremiah out of a muddy cistern, saving his life (Jeremiah 38:6-13). And as we touched on earlier, a black man named Simon from the African city of Cyrene in Northern Libya carried Jesus' cross beam to Calvary when Jesus could not do it Himself due to tremendous blood loss and severe physical exhaustion (Matthew 27:32-33). Simon had two sons, Alexander and Rufus (Mark 15:21) and this Rufus may have grown up to be the one that Paul wrote of in Romans 16:13 saying, *"Greet Rufus, chosen in the Lord, and his mother and mine."*

I kept reading and realized that Jesus ministered in the Gentile territories of Tyre and Sidon to a woman of Canaanite origin in Matthew 15:21-28. One of Jesus' twelve apostles was named *"Simon the Canaanite"* according to the King James Version of the Bible (Matthew 10:4, Mark 3:18). This glorious truth means that Jesus had an integrated staff before it was politically correct to do so! Simon was a descendent of the cursed enemies of the Israelites, yet Jesus acted affirmatively towards him and placed this minority on His leadership team. Simon's presence on Jesus' team spoke loudly of God's love and acceptance without anyone having to say a word. Jesus also referred to the Queen of the South who came to see and hear King Solomon (Matthew 12:42, I Kings 10:1-3). Africa is South of Jerusalem and this woman was called "the Queen of Sheba". She was an OT believer in God. What interested her in Solomon was what she heard about him concerning the name of the LORD (I Kings 10:1).

Africans were key leaders in the church of Antioch (Acts 13:1-3). There was Simeon who was also called "Niger". The word "Niger" means, "black" and he was addressed this way by the church. What's interesting is that many black men today still address each other that way by saying, "What's up, Black?" There was also Lucius of Cyrene in the church at Antioch. As mentioned, Cyrene is in northern Africa, which is modern day Libya. There were more Africans in leadership in the Antioch church in the first century than there are today in most congregations in America. These two men weren't on the custodial or grounds crew either. They were in visible leadership and they had real authority. That was important then and it's still crucial now in terms of establishing a church atmosphere that welcomes all people from the pulpit to the pew. Minorities will stay in integrated churches when they see leadership that looks like them. No wonder the disciples were called "Christians" first in Antioch (Acts 11:26). Jesus is truly put on display in the midst of ethnic diversity and empowerment racial reconciliation. Jesus must be real if He can bring Jews, Europeans, and Africans together in one local church. I believe He still has that same kind of power and desire today to make our churches look and function like the church in Antioch. Seattle's Antioch Bible Church under the leadership of Dr. Ken Hutcherson has worn the name well for over twenty-five years of exhibiting ethnic diversity.

WHAT COLOR WAS ADAM?

So where did all of this color in the Bible come from? If we believe the Bible it came from God through Adam. Knowing the true color of Adam may not be important to some of us, but it's a critical topic to a few of us that's been long overdue for an overhaul. If we start our reading and understanding of the Bible under the premise of lies or myths, that means our foundation for interpretation on everything else will be distorted and jaded as we go on in the Scriptures. As teachers, we must cease passing untruths and cultural biases onto our listeners causing them to interpret the Bible and live life through a worldview that does not include God's heart and intentions.

Every word of Scripture is inspired by God and should be interpreted soundly within its context (II Timothy 3:16-17). Biased exegesis based on racism was done in the past, and these faulty interpretations led to justifications for the enslavement and unjust treatment of Africans and their American descendents. Bad theology leads to bad sociology, but not only that, bad theology produces bad art and these images influence how people think. Art is supposed to imitate life, not reinforce questionable theological premises. Today in the 21st century, it may be politically correct in some churches to have non-white depictions of Adam and Eve, but that was not always the case. What color were Adam and Eve in printed Sunday school curriculum throughout the 1900's? They were white, and many white people that I've talked to say they don't care what color Adam and Eve happened to be. It is usually a non-issue for them because Adam and Eve have always been portrayed without question as being two white people with long, blonde hair and animals perfectly placed around them and their private parts in the Garden of Eden.

Let me tell you when their color matters. It would matter if you walked into a church lobby or a Christian bookstore today and saw a large display with a black, brown, Native, or Asian portrayal of Adam and Eve on it. After looks of bewilderment somebody would get a phone call. Ask kids across America of all ethnic groups to draw and color a picture of Adam and Eve, and the vast majority of them will draw them with Caucasian features. They will color Adam and Eve "white" using a "flesh tone" crayon to do it! Perception has become reality, and when these false ideals are forged in the minds of our children they usually breed a sense of superiority or inferiority.

"RED MAN"

Let's break down Genesis 2:7 that reads, *"And the LORD God formed man of the dust of the ground and breathed in his nostrils the breath of life; and man became a living being."* The English word "man" is the Hebrew word "adam". It literally means "of the ground" or "taken from red earth". In Genesis, "Adam" is both a general noun for "mankind" (Genesis 2:18) and a personal name for the first man (Genesis 2:19). The English word "dust" is the Hebrew word "aphar" which can mean "ashes", "powder", "dust", or "clay". The word "ground" is the Hebrew word "adamah" which means "red soil", "red ground" or "red clay".

Therefore Adam means "red man" or "man taken from red earth". Adam was a "red man of the earth". Adam could not have been white or a European; neither was he black. It would be safe to say that Adam was a man of color. If anything, Adam may have been what we would classify today as an "Indian", or less offensively, a Native American or a First Nation person. I pray the day will soon come when Americans will stop overlooking the original presence of the Red Man whether in the Scriptures or in America. This is still a hard pill to swallow, but God provides the water.

Adam in the Hebrew language is closely associated with the Hebrew word for "Edom" which means "red". Edom was another name for Esau and he was the eldest son of Isaac being so named because of his red hair (Genesis 25:25) and his love for red lentil stew (Genesis 25:30). The Hebrew culture insisted on parents naming their children after distinguishing physical features or pertinent historical occurrences. For instance, Moses means "drawer out". He was drawn out of the Nile River and he would draw God's people out Egypt (Exodus 2:10). In many respects our formal names describe and define who we are as well as what we will become.

Did the outer shell of dust make Adam a living being or did receiving breath from God make him a living being? It was Adam's spirit from God that made him a human and not his flesh. His soul/spirit was made in the image of God and not his body because God is Spirit (John 4:24). It must therefore be the goal of men to connect with each other on a spirit and soul level as we connect with God. This is what keeps us from being separated on a flesh level. Paul concluded that he would no longer judge anyone after the flesh because he foolishly did this with Jesus and missed the essence of who He was (II Corinthians 5:16). Let's stop judging by the color of skin and judge by spirit. As Dr. King so famously said in his I Have a Dream speech, "I have a dream that my four children will not be judged by the color of their skin but by the content of character".

GENETICS AND RACE

So-called racial distinctions are only minor variations among the people groups. Scientists have found that if one were to take any two people from anywhere in the world, the basic genetic differences between these two people would typically be 0.2% difference, even if they came from the same people group. The best tissue match for an organ transplant may come from someone of another "race". The only reason we think these differences are major is because we've been brought up in a society that has conditioned us to see differences negatively. Race has always mattered in America and it has mattered unfavorably. So far we have not been very successful at changing that perception.

Genetically speaking, the first couple had to have enough melanin in their genes to produce a vast array of skin tones. Melanin is a dark brown to black pigment in the skin that tans skin as it is exposed to sunlight. All people have the same kind of pigment in their skin called melanin. We just happen to have different amounts of it. Dark skinned people have more melanin and lighter skinned people have less. It is genetically impossible for little melanin possessing parents to give birth to dark skinned children. However the genetic possibilities to produce light or bright skinned people are inherent within dark skinned people. It makes scientific sense for Adam to have had a medium to dark, reddish complexion. He carried the genes for a wide amount of melanin so that he could be the ancestral father of all people groups with wide variations of skin tone. It would be impossible for a white Adam to have multi-toned peoples emanating from him. It was imperative for the first couple to be of a darker complexion because they housed within their genes the capacity to spawn children of various hues. It was always God's intent to have a variety of skin tones for the one human family!

Technically speaking, the Bible knows nothing about our modern day term "race". Although the NIV uses "race" in Romans 9:3, older translations like the KJV interpret the Greek word as "kinsmen" or "countrymen". The Bible only speaks of families, tribes, nations, descendents, generations, and peoples. Charles Darwin's book, <u>On The Origin of Species</u> and its later editions not only espoused evolutionary biology, but he also bred a racist philosophy that different groups or "races" of people competed and evolved at different times and rates, thus making some groups more like their ape ancestors than others. In his estimation, the black race evolved slower than the white race meaning that black people are not on the same plain intellectually or morally as white people. It was and still is believed that black people resemble apes in appearance, intelligence, sexuality, and athleticism. For years blacks have been called "porch monkeys", "baboons", "apes", and "gorillas".

BLACK IS BEAUTIFUL BABY!

God uses explicit detail when making and describing His people in the Bible. We know that Saul was tall and handsome (I Samuel 9:2) and that Zacchaeus was short (Luke 19:3). We know that David was ruddy or red complexioned, with bright eyes and good looking (I Samuel 16:12). We know that Goliath was uncircumcised and nearly 10 feet tall (I Samuel 17:4, 36). We know that Eli the priest was a heavy man (I Samuel 4:18) and that Ehud the judge was a left-handed Benjamite (Judges 3:14). Rachel was beautiful in form and appearance and her sister Leah had weak or delicate eyes (Genesis 29:17). Joseph was well built and handsome (Genesis 39:6) and the Ethiopians were dark and tall and they could not change their skin any more than a leopard could change its spots (Jeremiah 13:23).

God never wanted black people to be ashamed of their ebony skin. He wants us to be proud of it. As it says in Psalm 139:14 we should praise God for being fearfully and wonderfully made! Black is beautiful and black is biblical. In the Song of Solomon, the Shulamite woman proudly says, *"I am dark but lovely, O daughters of Jerusalem, like the tents of Kedar, like the curtains of Solomon"* (Song of Solomon 1:5).

Christians of all hues cannot be afraid to acknowledge beauty and skin color today. We're hesitant because we don't know what is politically correct anymore. History has proven that black people, with their various shades and tones of skin, are often viewed around the world as negative, inferior, and threatening. Americans in particular have been indoctrinated to fear the very dark black man because he is seen as evil or imposing. Therefore today, a lot of well-meaning white people go to the opposite extreme and say, "I don't see color". When white people say this they are devaluing the black person's color. A black person is not "clear" in color. Dogs may be colorblind but God is not colorblind, and He did not create us to be that way either. Any person's color, especially a black person's color, may be a description but it is no longer meant to be a definition or a limitation.

As a black man I absolutely love my God-given heritage. I am Christ-centered and Afro-sensitive. I love my course hair, my thick nose, and my full lips. I love certain aspects of my culture because Christ never called me to totally disengage from my humanity. In His sovereignty He placed me in my black family and my black skin without giving me a choice or asking for my opinion (Acts 17:26). He established my boundaries and decided when, where, how, and to whom I would be born. This is cause to celebrate. I am confident because God has a specific plan for my life written in His book

(Psalm 139:16). By faith I am living out each sentence, page, and paragraph under His divine power and foreknowledge. A Jewish Savior named Jesus rescued me from my sin and declared me righteous in His sight. He adopted me and now I am a co-heir with Him in thc kingdom (Romans 8:17). I am not an accident. I am a provident incident of divine craftsmanship. I am not cursed. I am blessed. God loves me. I love me, and you should, too!

4. WHITES ONLY! BLACKS ONLY!

The Underground Railroad that existed in the 19th century during the days of American slavery is the greatest and most productive example of "empowerment racial reconciliation" between blacks and whites that this nation has ever known. The obvious need for the freedom of America's millions of African slaves went far beyond the founding father's original idealism to form a more perfect union. Nevertheless, freedom for all, including the slave, became our nation's new conscience and lifeblood, and it would slowly begin to be accomplished through organized underground channels.

ALL ABOARD!

The Underground Railroad partnered blacks and whites together in ways that were unheard of in that day. Blacks and whites had to trust each other without fully knowing each other, but they could do so because their mission was mightier than their apprehensions. Much of this movement occurred against the backdrop of night and in the face of great, impending danger. Blacks and whites placed their lives and livelihoods in one another's hands. They didn't have a written script but they did have an underlying code of operation and an overriding determination to gain freedom from injustice and slavery.

Whites took risks and built secret compartments in their homes with the slave in mind. Blacks took risks and ran away from their masters fully knowing the consequences if ever caught. White "station masters" took risks and opened their homes to fleeing black "passengers" in the middle of the night. Free blacks as well as Native Americans assisted along the routes to free states in the North and to Canada. But white families in particular put the comforts of their families in jeopardy as they lived under the fear that any day some well meaning, "Christian neighbor" could turn on them if their secret ever got out. Even still, courageous whites provided for black people's safety and sustenance, demonstrating that they had a love for the poor that cost them something. Because of the Underground Railroad's success laws were soon passed like the Fugitive Slave Law of 1850. The law prohibited whites from assisting and aiding slaves escaping for freedom even in free states. But unjust laws have always been meant to be broken (Acts 4:18-20) and the abolitionists continued their work through the end of the Civil War in 1865.

The Underground Railroad tells us that there have always been sympathetic whites stationed along the costly road of empowerment racial reconciliation with blacks. Most people know about the great Harriet Tubman and how she was able to conduct the freedom of hundreds of slaves through the railroad. Some may know about former slave and freedman William Still who has been called the father of the Underground Railroad. But how many of us know that Wild Bill Hickok was also a white abolitionist? His father's farm in Homer, Illinois was one of the stops on the Underground Railroad. In fact, he learned his shooting skills protecting the farm from slave catchers. Then there is the Rev. John Rankin, a white Presbyterian minister who became Ohio's first and most active conductor. His house on a hill and the light that would shine from it provided the escaping slaves the knowledge and courage to cross the icy waters of the Ohio River towards freedom. His writings challenged his own brother to refrain from owning slaves and join the abolitionists. Rankin also impacted William Lloyd Garrison and Harriet Beecher Stowe. Black people need to know, applaud, and teach these facts. Blacks hate it when we are left out of biased, one-sided, revisionist history books; therefore we should be quick to tell the whole story ourselves. There are certain truths that black people authenticate when brought to light just as when white people bring certain stories and facts to bear.

THE POWER OF 7,000

I contest that God has majority, white folks in the minority who are mindful to help minority, black folks. God always has a group of white people who have not bowed the knee to prejudice and institutional racism like the majority seemingly has, especially in the early days of our nation's development. But God always has a remnant. Remember when Elijah thought he was alone in his effort to stand up against Baalism and rid the land of its evil influences in I Kings 19:10-14? Elijah thought he was fighting by himself, so God reminded him that he was not the only one making a stand for truth and justice. There were seven thousand others standing for God as well (I Kings 19:18). They may not have been well known to the public but they were well known to God. They may not have been famous and out front like Elijah, but they were just as effective and as necessary to the cause of God by operating underground and working behind the scenes.

It is historically inaccurate for blacks to say "all" white people are a particular, negative way. Blacks are often irritated when white people do that to us, so let's be sure not to have sweeping indictments towards them. The problem with categorizations is that we lump good people in with other people whom we deem as not good. When we make these sweeping indictments of a whole group of people, we end up hurting segments of that people who are unfortunately guilty by association. All white people aren't against all black people and all black people aren't against all white people. That can't be stated enough.

In fact, there's a great chance that "your own people" can do you more personal harm and destruction than other ethnic groups ever could. I have derogatorily been called nigger to my face far more times by malicious black people than by ignorant white people. I have had more black people try to hold me back academically and be jealous of my social progress than white people. Every black person is not my brother and every white person is not my enemy. My family, like Jesus taught, happens to be my brothers and sisters who do the will of the Father, and they come from all nations (Matthew 12:46-50). This means that God's family takes higher precedence and priority over my biological or ethnic family. Jesus lived and died this way. Shouldn't we, also?

GOOD WHITE FOLKS

It was a white man named John Brown who led a violent yet unsuccessful raid to free blacks from slavery in 1859 at Harper's Ferry, Virginia. He had zeal but it was not coupled with wisdom. Frederick Douglass and Harriet Tubman rejected his offer to join his militia. Douglass and Tubman chose to liberate their people through other means, but I wonder how many blacks actually know about abolitionist John Brown? How many blacks know about the relationship between William Lloyd Garrison and Frederick Douglass? How many blacks know about the genuine, interdependent relationship that Abraham Lincoln and Frederick Douglass respectfully had with one another? It was Douglass who urged Lincoln to strongly consider the reasons for allowing blacks to fight for the Union Army in the Civil War. In the book, A Team of Rivals: The Political Genius of Abraham Lincoln, the story is told from Frederick Douglass' perspective of his interaction with the president after Lincoln gave his second inaugural. Douglass quotes Lincoln as saying, "Here comes my friend Douglass. I am glad to see you. I saw you in the crowd today, listening to my inaugural address; how did you like it? You must stop a little, Douglass; there is no man in the country whose opinion I value more than yours. I want to know what you think of it." Douglass replied, "Mr.

Lincoln, that was a sacred effort." Lincoln's face lit up with delight and he said, "I am glad you liked it!" (p. 700)

Jesus said that people do good things because of the good that is stored up in their hearts (Matthew 12:35). Jesus also said that good trees bring forth good fruit (Matthew 7:17). There are white people who have demonstrated good fruits in regards to race relations because they have good roots in God, and I am not an "Uncle Tom" for saying that. And for the record, Uncle Tom was the main character and "Christ figure" in the book Uncle Tom's Cabin by Harriet Beecher Stowe. I have discovered that most of the blacks that look down on Uncle Tom have never read the book. Only God could use a white woman to write a book that would help provide the conscience that America needed to begin its quest towards ending slavery. When Abraham Lincoln met Mrs. Stowe he reportedly said, "So this is the little lady who started this new, Great War!"

Another white lady named Susan B. Anthony devoted her life in the 19th century to women's suffrage issues in the United States. She also included petitioning for the civil rights of African American women in the process. She sought the empowerment of all women, and not just white women. Another white lady named Mary White Ovington became involved in campaigning for civil rights in 1890 after hearing Frederick Douglass speak in a Brooklyn church. Ovington, along with two white men named William English Walling and Dr. Henry Moskowitz formed the basis for what would be the NAACP in 1909. When the NAACP was officially founded in May of 1910, Ovington was appointed as executive secretary. How many blacks, and whites for that matter knew that the NAACP was initiated and founded by three white people? I have a white lady in my church named Debbie French that started a ministry many years ago called Today's Choices that holistically empowers African women in Ghana, West Africa. Debbie, along with her co-founder and white sister-in-the-Lord, Pam Hawkins, have been greatly used by the Lord at home and abroad to affect lives for the kingdom of God.

I believe black people forget that there have always been white people who have been with us every step of the way fighting with us against slavery and segregation in the past. Granted, black people would like to see more white people making public stands today and not just providing the bulk of their support privately or financially. Underground Railroad whites may have been invisible but they were involved, and during the Civil Rights era of the 1950's and 60's, whites standing with blacks seemed to be a little more visible than they are today in the 21st century. Who can forget the murders of the three Mississippi civil rights workers in 1964? James Chaney was black, while Andrew Goodman and Michael Schwerner were Jewish young men. Unfortunately, most whites that publicly stand up today against racism are usually promoting a liberal agenda that has any and everything under its cloak of so-called human rights and diversity.

We need more whites to step up and be counted for. One of the reasons my work in the South has been successful is because I have always had strong, white brothers and sisters stand with me. Along the way there have been godly, white men like Rev. Scott Roley, Al Jaynes, Brandon Dyson, Steve French, Paul Riviere, John Brewer, Stu Southard, John Maguire, Dan Pitts, Mike McGlafflin, Kyle Cooksey, and Toby Mckeehan to name a few. So if anyone should ever ask or wonder, a lot of my closest friends are white! You may not know these men any more than you may know the men whose names are recorded in Nehemiah 3:1-32 that were instrumental in helping Nehemiah build the walls around Jerusalem. Nehemiah would have never made it without those men, and the above-mentioned men are instruments of God in my life that love me and are presently helping me to build the kingdom of Jesus and I am forever grateful for them.

It was a white man named Jerry Falwell, who in 1989 gave two of my friends and me scholarships when he saw our work in the inner cities through our rap group Transformation Crusade. Dr. Falwell told us that he regretted not taking the stand he should have taken during the Civil Rights era and that he wanted to redeem some of his shortcomings by financially supporting us through college and seminary. Another white man named Ken Harmon helped me buy my first house through an investment he made for me without my knowledge. A white man named Larry Warren allowed me to accompany him to Africa for my first trip there, and I was blessed to meet several African dignitaries due to his influence. A white couple sent my wife and I to Israel where a white Bible teacher from Texas named David Reagan totally impacted our lives while there. I can go on and on. I have been blessed to empower and be empowered by my white brothers and sisters in the Diverse Kingdom of God. Obviously, I have been hurt numerous times and in various cruel ways by white people, but the good far outweigh the bad. I refuse to judge or give up on the whole because of the ignorance of a few.

WHITE BROTHER WHERE ART THOU?

Conservative whites usually stay away from justice issues for fear of being lumped in with liberals. For instance, the situation that occurred in Jena, Louisiana in 2006-2007 where six black teenagers were convicted in the beating of a white student. Many in black communities throughout the country felt the black youths were punished too severely, with one defendant being tried and convicted as an adult and not as a juvenile. I believe this matter should have prompted more participation from the white community than it did. It was another missed opportunity to begin bridging the divide.

The majority of whites appear to be reluctant to speak out and make a stand in these moments against the machine. When blacks march in the overwhelming majority and speak alone it makes these things appear to be "black issues" and not justice issues. I understand that most white, conservative evangelicals don't care for Jesse Jackson and Al Sharpton's involvement in moments of social struggle. Many black people question their motives and tactics as well, but I have to give them credit. Jackson and Sharpton are usually present when injustices occur whereas prominent white ministers are typically missing in action.

I saw black people publicly respond when President Obama was portrayed as a shot gorilla in a NY Post cartoon in February 2009. I didn't hear of many white people's responses in the media that were equally offended. What I did hear was members of the white media implying that this was nothing to get upset about. If President Obama is portrayed as a gorilla, a slave in chains, or a witch doctor they consider it to be political satire and not demonstrations of racism. In spite of the coarse connotations, these mockeries are downplayed. I saw America become divided in 2009 by the episode between Harvard professor Henry "Skip" Gates and Sgt. James Crowley at Gates' home in Cambridge, Massachusetts. Gates was arrested in his own home when officers responded to an apparent break in. Gates was booked and eventually released. Granted, we'll never know what happened inside of Gates' house that day between these two men. But there is one thing for certain, what we heard from both is a microcosm of how race is viewed in America, and that is from two totally different perspectives. The truth must be somewhere in the middle and we'll only reach that place when grace can super abound over race. Both men represent the best of their respective fields, but I also believe both men acted poorly and out of character in the heat of that moment. As far the nation's response, it was obvious that there weren't many sympathetic white voices that emerged, attempting to understand Gates' frustration. On the flip side, there weren't many black voices that arose and sought to understand Crowley's position and procedure. It would take having beers on the White House lawn with the President to quell the ruckus.

The church should be ashamed of itself. Societal professionals with fractured lives can work out their racial tensions at a table around beer, but black and white Christians can't work their racial tensions out around the blood of Christ at the communion table of grace. Blacks and whites need to step together against injustice issues. It's more powerful and effective that way. More people see Jesus when we are together than when we are apart.

There was an incident at my children's school where a noose was found hanging in the boys' restroom along with hateful words aimed at Jews and African Americans. Two teachers approached me about helping out, one was black and the other was white. The great thing about the situation is that when I showed up at the school to confront this racial hate crime or spoke with television stations in my office, I had 800 people standing with me who were black, white, yellow, red, and brown. Together we were able to call attention to this matter as well as to offer our help to the kids who committed the crime and the kids who were offended by the crime. When lower income blacks show up in City hall meetings to petition for affordable housing it may not get much of a response. But when I can gather 200 black, white, brown, and yellow people to City Hall to petition for affordable housing it rattles more cages and has more potential to get the attention of the powers that be. We are stronger when we stand together.

BLACKS DON'T BLAME

For just as white people will never make progress racially as long as they continue to deny culpability for the gulf that exists today between blacks and whites, black people will never get anywhere either as long as we continue to blame white people exclusively for our situation. As long as blacks keep blaming whites, and whites keep denying or avoiding blame we'll never heal as a nation or a church. When we blame we never take responsibility. As long as it's someone else's fault it's never my fault. It's easier to point my finger at you than it is to point a thumb at myself. The natural tendency of man is to blame others, God, and the devil. Adam and Eve did this and so do we (Genesis 3:1-7).

Like Hosea the prophet said to his people Israel, I apply to African Americans, *"My people are destroyed for a lack of knowledge"* (Hosea 4:6). As with the Jews in Hosea's time, harlotry, adultery, and idolatry have plagued black people. Violence, materialism, and stubbornness unfortunately characterize us, and our primary problem as a people is not social or economical but spiritual (II Chronicles 7:14, Romans 10:2). "Black America" needs a revival.

Every ethnic group has a perennial blind eye or deaf ear. Most Jews are blind to their spiritual disposition (Isaiah 6:9-13). Whites are typically despondent and unaware of racial matters, and blacks tend to suffer for not taking personal responsibility. Black people have exclusively blamed slavery on the white man not realizing that African chiefs sold and traded Africans to Europeans in the first place. The chiefs gave the Europeans the authority and the personal guides to go inland into the bush and bring out captives to the shores to be placed on slave ships. It wasn't just the white man; Africans were responsible for the slave trade, too.

In the face of a growing drug epidemic in the 1980's black people said that they didn't own the boats or the planes that brought the cocaine and other drugs into our communities. That may have been true but it wasn't the white man selling it to our people on the corners and in the crack houses of our urban cities. We did that and just like the African chiefs of old, the love of money produced a root of evil that led us to sell our own people into slavery (I Timothy 6:10). We blame our family breakdown, black-on-black crime, poor education, jail status, and poor living conditions primarily on the white man and not enough on the black man. We are worshipping at the altar of materialism, uncleanness, and violence and we're reluctant to call each other out. Many of our churches are filled with homosexual spirits and not the Holy Spirit. We seemed to be richer when we were poorer.

When Bill Cosby called black people to the carpet for our irresponsibility to raise our children properly, he was immediately castigated by Michael Eric Dyson and others like him. Yes, the system is culpable but it is not totally responsible for our demise. We didn't accept systemic slavery in the past so why are we okay with spiritual slavery now? But in the spirit of Maya Angelou "We can still rise again." If we continue to blame the white man as the primary reason for our dilapidated condition we'll never improve as a people. Blame never leads to productivity. Although there has been and still is well-documented victimization of African Americans, we'll never experience victory if we maintain a victim's mentality. Victims are never victors and whiners never win. Black people can't allow the white man to have that much power over us. When we blame him we are giving him too much credit and this fallacy flies in the face of God's power to deliver and black strength that was forged in the furnace of suffering.

WHITE DENIAL

On the other hand, whites cannot deny their part historically if they want to make progress in race relations. Denial and apathy add fuel to the fire, and fury to the frustration. This generation of whites did not own black slaves but they have benefitted indirectly from a system and culture built on the notion of white dominance and supremacy. Whites still make more money per household than any other ethnicity in America and their net worth exceeds that of blacks, Latinos, Natives, and Asians. Studies have proven that whites are more likely to receive business loans from banks and better treatment in the marketplace and workplace. Statistics indicate that white people are more inclined to serve lesser sentences when convicted as opposed to blacks that are convicted of the same crime.

White brother, you can't historically kick my behind and then deny that you did it. You can't see me walking with a limp and then deny pushing me down the stairs. But neither can I start to heal and begin to walk upright as a black man, but then grab my crutches when it gets hard or when I want to complain or reject responsibility. If blacks and whites sit down together at the same table to play a game of cards, whites must admit that the deck was stacked against blacks for the first four hundreds years of the game of American life. The game was not fair and the rules made it difficult for blacks to win a hand or make a score. On top of that, the rules kept changing whenever black people started making progress. Conversely, blacks can't keep adding the perennial "race card" to the deck every time a tense matter arises between races. Every problem between people of different races is not always a race problem. Many times it is a people problem and not a prejudice problem. However, we all know prejudice people and racism still exist, but black people must be wise in their public declarations of determining what is a legitimate racial incident and what is just an incident. If you pull the race card all of the time you lessen the impact for when actual happenings occur.

As in the days of segregation, Jim Crow laws and signs were prevalent as the rule of the land. These signs told white and "colored" people where they could shop, drink, eat, lodge, sit, or go to the movies. Some places and entrances were for "Whites Only" and others were for "Blacks Only". Below I've listed some key principles and suggestions for blacks and whites living together in God's Diverse Kingdom. In addition to the Word of God, hang these principles over your heart.

PRINCIPLES FOR WHITES LIVING WITH BLACKS IN GOD'S DIVERSE KINGDOM

1) It is great to make strides in individual and personal relationships with black people. You must also be ready to see and confront racial injustice in

your family, your neighborhood, your school, your job, your church, the media, and in the mainstream.

2) Ask God to open your eyes to see and your heart to feel racial injustice perpetrated against minorities by the majority. If you think you can see already, Jesus says you are blind. Admit to God that you can't see and He will slowly begin to give you sight (John 9:40-41).

3) Don't say that you are "color blind". Blacks know that you are implying that race is not an obstruction to you like it once was in America. Levelheaded blacks know that you mean well but that utterance can be offensive, and besides, it's unrealistic. We are never unaware of the color of the person with whom we interact. America has built race into all of our sub-consciences like it or not.

4) Be a student of history. For instance, learn why there is a black history month and why blacks felt there was a need to create a Black Entertainment Television station in the 1980's. Don't just dismiss these things without proper investigation.

5) Be willing to voluntarily and intentionally place yourself under minority leadership. You may want to consider joining a church that is led by African American leadership or take a class offered by a black teacher. Be sure to expose your children to dynamic minority leaders who operate outside of the sports and entertainment fields.

6) Read books written by minority authors and offer them to your colleagues. You won't agree with every tenet as with any other book you read. Hopefully there will be some insights gained as a result of having an open mind.

7) Resist trying to be a white savior for ethnic minorities in the United States and abroad. Free yourself by reminding yourself that you cannot save anyone, but you can serve everyone. You are not the Christ, and don't let anyone guilt trip you into thinking it's all up to you because it's not. Deliverance is up to God.

8) If you are a lover of the South, be sensitive to how you promote your passion for history and the Civil War. Realize that the vast majority of black people find the Confederate Flag offensive and agree with Frederick Douglass that the Civil War was fought primarily over the issue of slavery and not the classic "state's rights" position. You don't have to agree with that position but when you adamantly oppose this perspective that the war was not fought because of slavery, you are in essence saying that black life was not important

enough to fight for. It's hard enough to pinpoint exact reasons for modern day wars like the ones in Vietnam and Iraq, so please be respectful in discussing a war that occurred almost 150 years ago.

9) Be willing to acknowledge and confess the sins of your white forefathers even though you or your family never sinned by personally owning slaves (Daniel 9:4-19). As you read Daniel's prayer ask yourself, "What sins did Daniel commit for him to have to confess?" Acknowledge that American slavery and segregation were wrong and that many whites benefit today from our tilted society simply based on their skin color. Things are a lot better than they used to be but there is still a lot of room for improvement and progress.

10) When you don't know, don't try to act like a know it all. When you don't understand, don't be quick to criticize black culture. Instead, be quicker to ask questions rather than assuming you know the answers. Be quicker to hear and slower to speak.

11) Develop authentic, ongoing, honest, and open relationships with blacks and other minorities. Have them over to your home and spend time in their homes. Break bread and share the gospel as well as your lives with one another (I Thessalonians 2:8).

12) Stand up and speak up when there are known crimes, injustices, and ill treatment perpetrated against minorities simply because of the color of their skin. Silence from whites, especially white clergy during battles for civil rights is unacceptable (Micah 6:8). Resisting and overthrowing injustice is the Christian's call regardless of race. It's what we do (Proverbs 29:7 NIV)!

13) Open your eyes to see ethnic variance in the Scriptures. Get rid of caricatures in your home or church that portray Jesus and other Bible characters as modern era white people. Realize that these images continue to reinforce the myth of white domination and supremacy.

14) Be willing to learn history and culture from minorities. You may discover that your teachers misled you or purposefully lied to you by changing or leaving out segments of history so as to lift up whites in a more favorable light.

15) Don't be so quick to say that shameful incidents in society involving minorities are not racially motivated situations. You will rarely hear white people say or admit that racism sometimes plays a part in matters of societal injustices. Don't downplay the negative experiences blacks undergo at the hands of whites. Just because you don't see it or have never experienced it

doesn't mean that it is not true or that it didn't occur. A sense of sympathy develops best when you have authentic, growing, and ongoing relationships with minorities.

16) Be willing to let go of your ignorance and stop using the word "nigger" and other demeaning and derogatory terms in private. When you hear your friends or family use it, correct them.

17) Realize that the reality of race in America is at the forefront of the day-to-day mindset, life experiences, and conversations of the majority of black people. Although you may not be able to comprehend this it doesn't mean that it's not another man's mindset and experience. Never tell a black person that you know exactly what they're going through. Until you've walked extensively in community with black people you should be careful. Never tell a black person that he or she should just "get over the race thing". You will come across as being insensitive, arrogant, and unfortunately typical.

18) Don't neglect or despise other minorities as they grow numerically or advance socially. The continent of North America did not originally belong to white people. As the Statue of Liberty in New York stands facing the Atlantic Ocean beckoning for huddled masses yearning to breathe free, she must not forget the huddled masses already behind her currently suffering to make it in our cities and reservations.

19) If you adopt minority children make sure that you thoroughly study and continue to learn about your adoptive child's history and culture. Don't assume you know everything already, and when it comes to matters of doing their hair, please seek out professionals that have experience on your child's course and style of hair until you get to the stage where you can adequately do it yourself. Bring your adopted children around people from their race and heritage. It will benefit both of you.

20) Be wise enough to know that the images you see in the media and on television that often cast black people in negative and stereotypical vantage points should not be the primary basis through which your sociology is developed.

21) Don't assume that Al Sharpton and Jesse Jackson speak for all black people because they don't. However, you will know that you've really begun to grow in cross-ethnic relations when you can hear any good points these two men may make in a speech or confirm any good actions they may perform in civic efforts.

22) When speaking of the origins of America and the need to return back to the ideals, morals, and principles of our founding fathers, be mindful that not all blacks or Native Americans feel the same way. The "good old days" weren't so good for minorities. The obvious contradictions and hypocrisies in the lives of white Christians' who owned, abused, raped, and benefitted financially from slavery, and who robbed, exploited, and mistreated Native Americans, and stood for and violently enforced segregation makes the claims of America being established as a Christian nation of little effect.

23) Keep in mind that although the Confederate Flag is a historic symbol of our country's heritage to most whites, it is also a hateful and threatening symbol to most blacks, especially when they saw it being carried by hate groups like the Ku Klux Klan and the Arian Nation. This may be a call to apply Paul's admonition of denouncing your Christian liberty so as not to put a stumbling block in your brother's path (Romans 14:1-21). Sure the Confederate flag belongs in a museum, but does it belong on your bumper, hat, or t-shirt (Romans 15:2)?

24) Don't stop reaching out to ethnic minorities if you have had some bad experiences with one or two people in the past. Don't indict a whole people group based on the behavior of a few.

PRINCIPLES FOR BLACKS LIVING WITH WHITES IN GOD'S DIVERSE KINGDOM

1) Channel your anger at the right things. Be angry and don't sin (Ephesians 4:30). White people aren't your problem (Ephesians 6:10-18) and they surely aren't your enemies according to the Bible (I Peter 5:8).

2) Don't judge all white people as being categorically the same because of the ignorance of a few. And in your judging, be careful not to judge the hearts and motives of others, for only God is authorized to do that (John 5:22).

3) Don't blame white people in general for you or your people's misfortunes and lack of progress. Take personal responsibility for your actions both good and bad. When you are around black people who are casting blame, intolerance, and hatred towards whites, be willing and ready to confront them and correct them.

4) If white people don't support government initiatives like affirmative action or financial reparations from slavery, it doesn't necessarily mean they are racists. So don't take it personal. It may simply mean they have different perspectives on these matters. Like you, they are entitled to their own opinions.

5) Be objective and willing to criticize your own people when they are wrong. This admonition includes challenging so-called "black leaders". Don't just support leaders simply because they are black, and don't insist that criticism of President Obama is an affront against him strictly because he's black. We must all be objective without being easily offended.

6) Realize that every black person is not your brother and every white person is not your enemy. A black person may discourage your future more than any white person ever will.

7) Know the past, feel the past, and move on from the past. Realize that no modern day scenario will be adequate to completely atone for, undo, repay, repair, or redeem past racial injustices perpetrated against people of African descent.

8) Be a student of your history and read books about your ancestors that made a difference and refused to quit. Consider learning about Harriet Tubman, George Washington Carver, Booker T. Washington, Charles Drew, Jackie Robinson, Sojourner Truth, Madame CJ Walker, Jesse Owens, Richard Allen, and Phyllis Wheatley to name a few.

9) Be willing to forgive white people in general or one's who personally offend you whether they ask for forgiveness or not (Luke 23:34).

10) Be willing to step in and be surrogate parents to black youth. Take care of the needs of your community by first taking care of the children. Be a father to the fatherless and a mother to the motherless.

11) Remember all of Dr. King's "I Have a Dream" speech and legacy and not just parts of it. Dr. King talked about blacks and whites walking hand and hand and sitting down together at the table of brotherhood.

12) Remember Malcolm X's eventual evolution towards racial harmony near the end of his life and not just his early years that were filled with rage, social segregation, threats of violence, and the prominence of the black man.

13) Stop making excuses and stop being a victim. Victims never experience victory.

14) Don't be ashamed for being black. God isn't ashamed of your blackness. He made you that way and created you for His glory. Love yourself. It's biblical (Matthew 22:39).

15) Don't jump to conclusions when negative events occur in the mainstream culture involving black and white people being at odds. Wait to get the whole story before overreacting or even commenting.

16) Hold the race card and play it only when the matter is legitimate. Pull it to bring awareness and justice and not to get preferential treatment or to bring shame.

17) Be free from thinking that you represent or speak for the entire race of black people when in the presence of white people. White people have no such concern. They view themselves as individuals and not as a group for the most part.

18) Do not use derogatory, racially charged language when referring to white people, whether in anger or in jest (Ephesians 4:29).

19) Acknowledge that there have always been white people sympathetic to the cause of black freedom and equality and we would not be where we are today had it not been for good-natured white people assisting us.

20) Don't be afraid to identify publicly with white people, especially when you are around black people.

21) Refrain from using the word "nigga", even around other black people. Regardless of the context, this term is a stumbling block to the cause of Christ (Romans 14:13-16).

22) Concern yourself with getting your education, speaking well, and not agreeing with all things black. These things are not equivalents with being white. Education is not "a white thing". Our enslaved ancestors never thought that way and neither should we. They did whatever it took to learn to read and to be articulate in the broader society and so should we.

23) Don't assume that Rush Limbaugh, Ann Coulter, Sean Hannity, and Bill O'Reilly represent all white conservative views across the board because they don't. You know you are growing in diversity if you can hear any good points they may make.

24) When you see white people trying to make inroads into community with you don't deny them, ridicule them, or be rude to them. Extend your hands to them.

THE JESUS TRAIN

It's time for blacks and whites to work together again like we did in the days of the Underground Railroad. It's time to lay aside our differences that divide and come together around the history, the destiny, and the Christ that unites us all. It's called the Diverse Kingdom of God and all of God's people need to get ready. The Jesus Train is not riding underground anymore. You have to board it above ground now because its riders are not ashamed of Christ, His gospel, or His Kingdom.

The Jesus Train is gaining steam! Can you hear it? Do you see it? Do you want to ride? The Jesus Train is departing from your house and it will ride all across America making stops in all kinds of neighborhoods to pick up all of your neighbors regardless of race. Do you have your ticket? Have you gotten onboard?

5. PETE EAT THE MEAT

Sometimes it takes a while for us to learn what the Lord is trying to teach us. He is very patient with us because He knows we don't always get the point the first time He communicates His will and His purposes to us. And guess what? The apostle Peter was no exception either.

There were many things about Jesus that Peter didn't fully understand until after Christ had resurrected and the Holy Spirit came on the day of Pentecost (Acts 2:1-21). Even though Jesus spoke constantly about His death and resurrection beforehand, Peter still wondered what the empty tomb meant (Luke 24:11-12, John 20:9). He didn't even believe the women's testimony after they said they had seen the resurrected Jesus. You think Peter would have understood the ramifications of the resurrection when you consider the lashing Jesus gave him in Caesarea when Peter tried to deter Christ from dying (Matthew 16:21-23). From where we sit it's easy to criticize Peter's foolhardiness.

There was also another aspect of the kingdom that Peter didn't get initially and that was how Jesus' death on the cross tore down the dividing wall between Jews and Gentiles (Ephesians 2:14). In some of His last words to His followers before ascending to heaven Jesus made it clear that He wanted His disciples to reach out to other nations and not just the Jews. This was in 30 AD (Matthew 28:19-20, Acts 1:8). Peter, like the other early disciples, hesitated when it came to following Jesus' example and orders to minister to the Gentiles. Culture was obviously greater than Christ's commands. Historians date the events in Acts 10 to have occurred around AD 39 or 40. This means Peter didn't move in obedience for 10 years from when the Master originally gave the Great Commission to make disciples of all nations.

But later is better than never and the episode in Acts 10 serves as Peter's personal awakening to multi-ethnic ministry and cross-racial relationships. It has been called the "Gentile Pentecost" because of its similarities to the Jewish believers' Pentecost in Acts 2. This portion of Scripture tells the story

47

of how a European soldier named Cornelius comes to faith in Christ through Peter's evangelistic efforts. Peter opened the door of the heavenly kingdom to Cornelius, and Cornelius was used by God to open the door of Peter's heart to see and experience God's Diverse Kingdom.

There are several principles to be gained from Acts 10 concerning biblical diversity. In fact, I call these principles **"The Six BE Vitamins of God's Diverse Kingdom"**. B Vitamins play important roles in cell metabolism for the human body. B Vitamins maintain healthy skin and muscle tone, enhance the immune and nervous systems' function, and reduce the risk of pancreatic cancer. There are eight B Vitamins for the human body and six for the body of Christ when it comes to Kingdom Diversity.

VITAMIN B-1: BE PRAYERFUL

There is no move of God without prayer. Prayer was the initial instrument to begin breaking down the cultural and racial walls of division. Cornelius, an unsaved Gentile, was a seeker of God. He was a good man but he was not a saved man. God saw Cornelius responding to what little illumination he had spiritually and decided to send him more revelation concerning the gospel (Acts 10:1-7). Cornelius put himself in position to hear from God because whenever we talk to God through prayer God also speaks back to us. This means that prayer is not just talking to God, prayer is also listening to God. God has something very important to say to us, but if we don't pray, we will not hear what it is.

As a result of seeking the face of God, God responded by sending Cornelius a vision of an angel (Acts 10:2-7). Angels are messengers of God who come from heaven and reveal God's will to certain individuals at crucial moments. Nowadays, God primarily reveals His will to us through prayer and the Holy Scriptures. In this particular episode of special revelation, the angel knew Cornelius' name and the spiritual journey he was on. The angel gave Cornelius specific instructions, including the name and location of Peter. What's interesting is that the angel didn't give Cornelius the gospel message. He reserved that privilege and responsibility for Peter to do (Acts 10:6) because God's plan was for the two men to meet and empower each other.

If you are burdened by the lack of authentic multi-ethnic relationships in your life, your church, your business, your neighborhood, or your school, you need to pray and fast (Acts 10:30). Prayer and fasting show God that we are serious to the point of not feeding the flesh for a few days in order to grow in the Spirit. Fasting magnifies our voice in God's throne room (Isaiah 58:4) and increases our ability to hear from God. It was prayer that got the ball rolling for these two men and not a program or an event. While Cornelius was praying in Caesarea, Peter was also praying to the same God thirty miles away on the roof of Simon's house in Joppa. God spoke to Peter specifically in prayer just like the angel spoke to Cornelius.

Peter, who may have been fasting also, was given a vision through a trance that he fell into. God used a sheet containing "unclean" animals in the Jewish diet as a way of communicating the grace of the new covenant. Under the new covenant, Jesus declared all foods as clean (Mark 7:19) meaning that the Jews were no longer under the restrictions, requirements, or repercussions of the Mosaic and ceremonial laws of the old covenant. They were now free to eat the meat of animals once declared unclean. Jesus used the vision for the acceptance of the animals to declare to Peter and the Jews that they can now accept the "unclean" Gentiles because Jesus would make them clean through the same blood sacrifice He made the Jews clean.

Everything begins with prayer and everything is sustained through prayer. Prayer is not *a* work of the ministry. Prayer is *the* work of the ministry. God reveals His will through prayer and God will bring different men together through prayer. Before we had our first church service in the fall of 1995 we prayed together periodically throughout the spring and summer months of that year. I saw from the prayer meetings those who were interested in this Diverse Kingdom vision.

VITAMIN B-2: BE OPEN

After being prayerful, we then have to be open to seeing God's timing. Right after Peter stopped praying God allowed the men sent from Cornelius to show up at Simon's house. Notice that they stood at the gate and called out (Acts 10:17-18). They didn't just walk up to the door. There were cultural and ethnic boundaries in place in those days that the people observed. Peter knew God was up to something because the Holy Spirit spoke to him immediately and told him that it was okay to go with the men because He had sent them (Acts 10:19-20).

In the book Experiencing God, Christian authors Henry and Richard Blackaby are quoted as saying, "When you labor where God is already at work, He accomplishes His purposes through you" (p. 34). Throughout this landmark book of discerning the will of God, the message resounds to find out where God is at work and join Him. Too often we ask God to bless what we're doing when He wants us to do what He's blessing. God was moving that day with Peter and Cornelius. Like Rick Warren said in his book <u>The Purpose Driven Church</u>, Peter decided to "recognize a wave of God's Spirit and ride it." (p. 14) When God makes a wave in your life, church, business or ministry—hold on! You are in for a very exhilarating experience! I am a witness that when you are open to what God is doing He will take you to places of wonderment that are far beyond your wildest dreams. I never wanted to plant a church, yet alone a multi-ethnic one. However, I decided to be open to what God wanted and now I'm riding God's wave and couldn't be happier.

Another thing to consider is that Peter and the men Cornelius sent had to be open to doing what they had never done before. I'm sure Cornelius' men had never gone in search of a Jewish preacher before. For the first time in his life Peter let Gentiles into his abode to spend the night, and then together they got up and traveled the road to Caesarea together. Peter took six Jewish men with him (10:23, 11:12) so it makes me wonder what they talked about as they journeyed that road together? What did they eat? It took them two days to get to Caesarea (10:23-24) so where did they lodge together? And once they get to Caesarea Peter does what he's never done before and he goes into a Gentile's house. This was a move that brought both blessings and curses because the Jews in Judea criticized Peter for this (11:2-3).

If you keep doing what you've always done you will keep getting what you've always had. But if you want something different, be willing to do something different. Reach out and invite someone into your home of another ethnicity. Be willing to be the guest in someone else's home of another culture or ethnicity. Share meals together and share projects together. Don't rest until you have found that minority to fill your upper-level position. He or she is out there by the thousands.

What's funny about this story is that Peter told Jesus "No" three times (Acts 10:14-16). If there is anyone who should have learned his lesson about telling Jesus "No", it should have been Peter! He is the one who told Jesus that he wouldn't let Him die, which led Jesus to rebuke him and call him Satan (Matthew 16:22). In Luke 22:31-34 during the Lord's Supper, Peter also emphatically told Jesus that he wouldn't deny Him. Unfortunately we know he did deny Jesus three times (Matthew 26:69-75). In this encounter on the roof in Acts 10, Peter still has the nerve to tell Jesus what he won't do! Didn't he learn his lesson? Have we learned our lesson?

Jesus told Peter to eat meat that He had declared clean, but Peter said he wouldn't do it because he had never eaten anything common or unclean. In other words, Peter was being more kosher than Jesus. Peter had a "higher dietary standard" than Jesus Himself! What arrogance! What folly! Ecclesiastes 7:16 says, *"Do not be over righteous. Why destroy yourself?"* But watch this hypocrisy. Peter was at a tanner's house waiting for something to eat when he told Jesus that he wasn't going to defile himself. Peter was ceremonially unclean at that moment himself. He must have forgotten that Simon the tanner made his living skinning animals; therefore, according to Old Testament law Peter was unclean by virtue of his close association with animal carcasses on the premises (Leviticus 11:39-40).

Be open to seeing what God sees and to doing what God is doing. Be open to going where you've never gone before. Be open to not being overly righteous in your quest to experience the Diverse Kingdom. Don't be high-minded and judge other people's lives and cultures while having a blind eye to your own culture's shortcomings.

VITAMIN B-3: BE HUMBLE

Racism in its simplest form is an abuse of power based on race. It is an intentional and often underlying and invisible system of advantages and disadvantages built strictly on race. When one group of people has the majority of the power, the resources, the wealth, and the opportunities, and they intentionally refuse to fairly share these assets with people of other ethnicities—that is racism. Prejudice is more of a personal offense whereas racism is more of a systemic offense. A person can be prejudice towards other ethnic groups but he or she may not be a racist because they may lack the systemic power to persecute or penalize others of another race. For instance, a white banker may have strong, negative, personal opinions about ethnic minorities but he still gives those minorities loans when they qualify in a non-biased process. He may be prejudiced but he's not a racist because he's motivated by green. On the other hand, a racist banker is one who denies giving loans to minorities or he makes the loan application process highly complex or impossible for other ethnicities to qualify so as to keep them from becoming empowered.

Because of America's early history, political and economic power was vested primarily in the hands of white Europeans and their descendents. Laws were passed and enforced to keep this imbalance in place for hundreds of years and it would take the passing of new laws to slowly begin changing the system. Ethnic minorities who managed to beat the system in the 1800's and 1900's of this country's development were the rare exception and not the norm.

51

Their progress made them targets of harassment and persecution by racist whites.

Pride is at the root of racism, but the beautiful thing is that racism cannot survive where there is humility. Christians are encouraged to esteem others as better than themselves (Philippians 2:1-4), so if we all spent time lifting others up, no one would feel superior or inferior. Even though America was built on two notions: 1) the superiority of the White male, and 2) the inferiority of ethnic minorities, especially the black race. The gospel in action breaks down these false notions if we believe it and act on it.

If we're honest we all wrestle with pride from time to time because we all wrestle with sin. The minute we think we don't have trouble with pride is the minute we have pride. If you move a halo a few inches down it becomes a noose. Pride and a lack of humility is a great detriment to kingdom ministry of any kind, but especially to multi-cultural, multi-ethnic, and multi-economic ministry.

When Peter walked into Cornelius' house he did not come in with a condescending spirit, a haughty look, or with his nose up in the air. He didn't come in with a chip on his shoulder. He didn't come in thinking he was God's gift to the Gentiles or that he was smarter than Cornelius. He came into the house so humbly that when Cornelius fell down at his feet to worship him (Acts 10:25) the Bible says Peter refused and *"… lifted him up, saying, 'Stand up; I myself am also a man'"* (Acts 10:26).

Peter demonstrated through that one action and that one statement that he was not superior to Cornelius. He saw Cornelius as his equal. Peter physically and personally lifted Cornelius up, dignifying him and recognizing his manhood by calling him a man. Before this vision happened Peter may have called Cornelius an unclean dog. He may have enjoyed the thought of having the "oppressor" down at his feet bowing in reverence, but God had done a work in Peter's heart through the vision. You see, when God does a work in you, the results are immediate. No one should have to wonder if God touched your heart. It should be obvious. You may have once called white people certain names or viewed Hispanics in a negative way, but once God moves on you, those old ways have to move out. Therefore be humble like Jesus and lift your brother up regardless of his color or ethnicity.

VITAMIN B-4: BE AWARE

Now that Peter had humbled himself he was ready to learn some things. Humble people are teachable people. It's impossible to learn when your pride makes you think you know everything there is to know. We learn from Peter that the first act of recovering from sins of race and prejudice is to become aware of the fact that racism is a deadly germ still inherent within each of us, and it's present in the systems in which we operate. Racism is in the air of the culture that we breathe subconsciously every day. We need a gospel gas mask of truth, love, and prayer to keep us from breathing it in constantly.

Peter had a race germ in his heart because he said to Cornelius, *"You know how unlawful it is for a Jewish man to keep company with or go to one of another nation. But God has shown me that I should not call any man common or unclean."* (10:28) For Peter to call Gentile people unclean was a blind spot he had until God showed him otherwise. Peter didn't see his sin until he saw the vision. We all have ethnic blind spots and until God shows us we won't see them, and if we think we don't have them Jesus can never heal us from them.

Peter also said there were social and ethnic partitions built into the culture that Cornelius knew about. Peter said to Cornelius, *"You know how unlawful it is for a Jewish man to keep company with or go to one of another nation."* (Acts 10:28) There were cultural laws in place that for the most part the people adhered to when it came to interacting with people of other nationalities. This was not God's law etched in OT Scripture. If that were the case, Jesus would have broken this so-called law and disqualified Himself as the Messiah because He kept company with other ethnic groups (Mark 7:24-30). This was a cultural "Jim Crow" law that the Jews exalted over the law of God and ultimately over the gospel. We do the same thing when we draw cultural boundaries around interracial dating and marriage. When we talk about illegal immigration we often leave the Scriptures as we share our opinion. We have areas where we exalt the culture's position over the Christian standard.

Peter went on to say in Acts 10:34, *"In truth I perceive that God shows no partiality."* The NIV puts it this way, *"I now realize that God is no respecter of persons."* For Peter to realize this now meant that he didn't realize this principle before, even when he walked with Jesus. Jesus taught on the inclusion of all people in His Diverse Kingdom, but Peter evidently wasn't listening. Jesus modeled the Diverse Kingdom through his outreach to Gentiles, but Peter evidently wasn't watching. But nearly ten years later Peter finally had his "now moment" in Acts 10 where he could see what he had never seen before as it pertained to race, race relations, and racism in various institutions.

Your "now moment" is when the lights come on and you begin to see what you've never seen before. You begin to hear what you've never heard before and you begin to feel what you've never felt before when it comes to race and racial issues. You no longer laugh at jokes that you used to laugh at. The mistreatment of minorities by your family, friends, and society, all of a sudden begins to bother you. You start to look for ways to open up access for other people groups to join you in your business endeavors and church fellowships. The indiscretions, inconsistencies, and injustices perpetrated against people simply because of the color of their skin or economic status infuriates you. When you have your "now moment" you begin to stand up and speak up to your own ethnic group when necessary. You are willing to be ridiculed and rejected if it comes down to that.

This passage tells me that it is possible to walk with Jesus in the flesh for a number of years and watch Him minister across ethnic and cultural lines and still subscribe to personal prejudice and racism. Before this episode, Peter obviously didn't see this as a sin so that means he must have felt God was ok with his thoughts, feelings, and philosophy of race relations. Peter ascribed to God his personal prejudice and preferences, and those mindsets are reinforced when you only stay with your kind.

Just because you read a book on racial reconciliation, go to a multi-ethnic church, visit Africa or Ireland, marry across ethnic lines, and have a black friend or a white friend doesn't mean that you get it. Through my own personal experiences, I believe it is more difficult for white believers to have their "now moment" than it is for ethnic minorities. Why is that? For black people and other ethnic minorities, race is at the forefront of our existence everyday and we talk about it boldly because we live it. We have no choice. We can't escape it. For whites there could be the blinding myth of white innocence that comes from the myth of white supremacy, or it could be the fear of getting ostracized from society once your true heart speaks. Christian white people are quick to join Paul's sentiments and admit to being the chief of sinners in every area but they are usually slow in admitting they have the germ of racism and prejudice in their hearts (I Timothy 1:14).

There are grave societal consequences if a white person admits to struggling with prejudice or racism. There is a strong possibility that that white person will be written off, judged harshly, and lumped into a category with hateful, outspoken, and proven white racists. It is hard to shake the label of "racist" once you are called that, so the best thing is not to publicly admit your fears, sins, concerns, and issues that you have about other people groups. It is this silence that frustrates many ethnic minorities that are trying to bridge the gap in race relations. Silence is seen as apathy. A lack of confession is seen as insincerity or arrogance.

If an apostle who walked with Jesus for three and half years needed to have a "now moment" of racial awareness, who are we to say we don't need one? This man not only walked with Jesus, but he preached and had thousands respond to Jesus. He performed miracles, raised the dead, was a pillar in the early church, and he wrote Scripture under the inspiration of the Holy Spirit. But even still, it took a specialized vision from Jesus for Peter to awaken from prejudice. What is it going to take for you and for me? It begins with us telling Jesus that we are blind and we can't see and we need Him to give us sight (John 9:39-41). And by the way, Jesus answers this prayer best in the context of ongoing, multi-ethnic community.

VITAMIN B-5: BE BLESSED

When Peter and Cornelius moved in unquestionable obedience God moved in unusual blessedness. John Maxwell put it this way in his book <u>Running with the Giants</u>, "God wants to be our partner throughout life. Too often we are tempted to either carry the entire load ourselves or give everything to God and do nothing. God doesn't like either strategy. Sometimes He moves before us and sometimes after us, but He won't move without us. Without God… we cannot. Without us…God will not. (p. 60)"

The Holy Spirit poured out a blessing in Caesarea that would forever change the scope of Christianity. The Holy Spirit baptized these Gentiles and placed them into the body of Christ (I Corinthians 12:13). A new chapter was written in Christian history as a Jewish leader and a Gentile convert each discovered something significant about God at work in them selves and in each other. Cornelius, the European Gentile, needed Peter, a former fisherman, to bring him the gospel so that he would know the way of salvation. On this day, Peter, a Jewish preacher, needed Cornelius, a military man, and his salvation experience to overthrow his personal prejudice by proving that God had indeed included Gentiles in His plan of redemption.

That day the Holy Spirit brought about an unusual blessing. The Holy Spirit is mentioned 5 times in Acts chapter ten (verses 19, 38, 44, 45, and 47). When the Holy Spirit moves, He takes over. He took over Cornelius and his relatives. He took over Peter, and He took over the gathering in that house. The questions are: Will the Holy Spirit take us over? Will he take our churches and Christian institutions over? Will He take our homes over? Will He take our relationships over? Will He take our agendas over?

VITAMIN B-6: BE READY

When God uses you to experience the blessedness of community across racial boundaries be ready to be persecuted by your own people because Peter was persecuted by the Jews (Acts 11:1-3). The Bible says the great apostle was "contended with". This verb means to be criticized sharply. Now if religious people of his own race jumped on Peter after a move of God what do you expect will happen to you? Don't think it strange of the fiery trials that will come upon you (I Peter 4:12).

The only thing Peter could do was to tell what happened. By telling the story he had a platform to testify and witness about what God had done because He was the catalyst behind it all. If the people had a problem with what happened then that meant they had a problem with God (Acts 5:38-39). Remember, Peter needed the Holy Spirit on the day of Pentecost to preach (Acts 2:4, 14) and he needed the Holy Spirit to fill him on the day when he was physically assaulted by the chief priests and Pharisees (Acts 4:5-22). He now needed the Holy Spirit to give him boldness to speak to his Jewish counterparts that were not present with him in Caesarea. Be ready to tell your story by the power of the Holy Spirit (Acts 11:4-17). Only God can change the hearts of people when the truth is spoken in love, and in this case God did just that (Acts 11:17-18).

After this great move of God you would think Peter would have arrived as "The Super Jewish Reconciler". With his cape flapping in the breeze, I can hear Peter saying, "Jewish brothers, I know the way to reconciliation! Follow meeeeeee!" Sadly, I have met too many white people that become "The Great White Reconciler" after they have had some success with ministering to minorities. These great, white hopes need to be taught all over again like Peter. Peter had to go back to "Reconciliation 101" when he found himself in Antioch a few years later in Galatians 2:11-14.

Peter was enjoying his freedom in Christ and he displayed it by eating foods once considered unclean and he ate with people once considered unclean. The vision and experience with Cornelius that God gave him in Acts 10 helped Peter grow in the continuum of race relations. But when his Jewish friends from Jerusalem came to Antioch Peter decided to withdraw from the Gentiles and their food. If this scenario happened in a lunchroom, Peter would have gotten up and switched tables. Peter reverted backwards, as we all have a tendency to do with other aspects of the faith. Imagine how the Gentiles must have felt when one of their spiritual leaders and pillar of the church was too ashamed to fellowship with them. The good thing is that the Apostle Paul was there in Antioch and he called Peter to account before everyone and rebuked him for not acting in accordance to the gospel (Galatians 2:14).

There's no mention that Peter changed from that rebuke, but I am quite sure he repented of his folly. When he wrote his first epistle in 63 AD to Jews and Gentiles alike, he called them *"living stones"* (I Peter 2:4-5). The beauty of this illustration is that stones vary in size, shape, mass, purpose, and color just like the body of Christ. Like Peter, be ready to be taught all over again. No one is an expert in race relations because no one has arrived in human relations. Stay teachable.

Finally, be ready to continue the work in the minority. According to Acts 11:19-21 only some of the Jewish believers continued in the work of preaching the gospel to Gentiles. The majority of the Jews wanted to stay with their own people so they made a conscience choice not to branch out. We must note that *"the hand of the Lord was with"* the ones that reached out and over to other people groups (Acts 11:21). Jesus said that He would be with any person or group of people willing to make disciples of all nations (Matthew 28:18-20). This unique and awesome experience of God's presence and the inexpressible joy of being with His diverse people are only for those who actually cross ethnic lines in order to love people with the hope of the gospel.

SECTION TWO

GOD'S DIVERSE KINGDOM COME THROUGH **CLASS**

"There is neither slave nor free…" Galatians 3:28b

1. THE PERPETUAL POOR

The kingdom of God is right side up even though it is considered to be upside down by people who are not a part of it. The message of Christ and His cross are considered foolishness to non-believers (I Corinthians 1:18). No wonder Jesus told Nicodemus in order for him to see and enter the kingdom he had to be born again (John 3:3, 5). God must give your heart, mind, soul, eyes, and ears a new start through His Spirit otherwise you'll never want to obey Jesus Christ (Philippians 2:13). Non-Christians, that is, the unconverted, can't see how or why we gladly honor God with our finances by giving to Him at church. They think it's strange that we choose to live sexually pure whether married or unmarried, and why through God's grace and strength we choose to live morally upright, abstaining from sinful activities that war against the soul (I Peter 2:11, 4:4). Many unbelievers just can't comprehend how and why we love our neighbors regardless of race, color, or creed.

The kingdom of God is completely opposite to this world's philosophy of life (I John 2:15-17), especially when it comes to wealth and material resources. The world tells us to "get all you can" as it pertains to money, whereas the kingdom of God says, "give all you can" (Luke 6:30, 38). That's the kingdom way to live because you can't take any of this stuff with you (Job 1:21), and as Randy Alcorn says about money in his book, The Treasure Principle, "You can't take it with you but you can send it ahead" (p. 17). The world "looks out for number one", while the kingdom says, *"look out for the interests of others"* (Philippians 2:4). That's living right side up. Money is merely a tool that we should never allow to make us fools.

THE GOSPEL OF THE KINGDOM

When John the Baptist came preaching the kingdom and the need for men to repent, he emphasized the necessity of treating people fairly and handling money and resources properly. He said, *"He who has two tunics, let him give to him who has none; and he who has food, let him do likewise"* (Luke 3:11). John said to the tax collectors who came to be baptized, *"Collect no more than what is appointed for you"* (Luke 3:13). To the soldiers John said, *"Do not intimidate anyone or accuse falsely, and be content with your wages"* (Luke 3:14). These are the fruits of our lives that are consistent with the profession of faith we made when we repented (Luke 3:8).

When wealthy Zacchaeus the chief tax collector had Jesus come to his house he was instantly changed by the encounter, and the evidence of that change showed up in how he immediately viewed his finances (Luke 19:1-10). Without being asked, Zacchaeus offered to give half of his goods to the poor. Knowing the law, he even offered to restore fourfold (Exodus 22:1) to anyone he may have cheated along the way in his pursuit to acquire wealth. In other words, he was willing to make financial reparations to anyone he may have cheated. This was a sign of his repentance. Jesus didn't stop him or try to persuade Zacchaeus towards a more "sensible" direction with his financial portfolio. No wonder Jesus went on to say, *"Today salvation has come to this house, because he also is a son of Abraham; for the Son of Man has come to seek and to save that which was lost"* (Luke 19:9-10).

Jesus began His earthly ministry by preaching the kingdom and His preaching was always coupled with mercy ministry to the poor and the sick (Matthew 4:23-25). He was anointed to preach the gospel to the poor and to heal the brokenhearted (Luke 4:18). The gospel of Jesus we preach today is not necessarily the gospel Jesus preached in His day. Evangelicals have emphasized the saving of individual souls but have historically done little when it comes to hands on involvement and empowerment of "the least of these" in our midst (Matthew 25:45).

I was once guilty of this indictment because I was trained to do ministry this way. I used to emphasize the saving of souls over holistic personal and community development. As a young minister, I could get people to pray a prayer of salvation but I didn't do much to better their life choices and conditions. I rode into town to do crusades and then rode out in a cloud of dust with more notches on my belt by way of conversions. I cared about saving souls but not about empowering people. I focused on getting them to heaven as opposed to giving them some heaven right now. I have since learned that preaching the gospel of the kingdom should never be separated from ongoing, hands on ministry to the poor, sick, rejected, and underserved of society.

MEEK NOT WEAK

Jesus lived by faith in God's ability to provide (Matthew 6:11). Being in an agrarian culture, Jesus and His disciples would oftentimes pick their food from trees (Mark 11:12-13) and from grain fields (Matthew 12:1). Their diet consisted of a lot of fish and bread (John 6:11, 21:6-12). Jesus was not rich financially but neither was He totally impoverished because He was healthy, educated, clean, and He ate regularly. Growing up as the Son of a carpenter (Mark 6:3), Jesus' family probably lived rather meagerly. Although He was born in a stable, wrapped in strips of cloth, and laid in a feed trough as a Baby (Luke 2:6-7), Mary and Joseph eventually went on to live in a house (Matthew 2:9-12). The gifts and money the wise men brought to the Child Jesus financed their impending trip and stay in Egypt (Matthew 2:13-15).

Jesus identified with and loved poor people, and poor people identified with Jesus and loved Him because He took upon Himself the form of a servant even though He was the King (Philippians 2:5-11). He came to serve and not be served (Matthew 20:28). He was not high-minded or pretentious. Jesus washed the dusty feet of His disciples, leaving us an example to follow (John 13:1-17), and He described Himself as having nowhere to lay His head (Matthew 8:20). He kept company with sinners and outcasts alike (Matthew 9:9-13) and He said that we should learn of Him because He was *"meek and lowly in heart"* (Matthew 11:29).

Jesus lived what He preached. He once said that a person's life does not consist in the abundance of his or her possessions (Luke 12:15). He spoke against the dangers of hording (Luke 12:13-20). He even said, *"What will it profit a man if he gains the whole world, and loses his own soul? (Mark 8:36)"* Jesus thought so much about money that He never carried it on His Person. Nowhere in the Bible does it say that Jesus personally carried or used money. In fact, when it came time for Him to pay the annual temple tax He had Peter get the money miraculously by fishing and finding it in a fish's mouth (Matthew 17:24-27). The Bible records how the disciples had a moneybag that Judas oversaw and sometimes stole from (John 12:6, 13:29), but it never says Jesus handled the money. When Jesus sent His disciples out to do local ministry among the people He sent them without money (Luke 10:3-4) so they could experience living by faith as they ministered to the poor, healed the sick, and proclaimed the nearness of God's kingdom (Luke 10:9).

By today's standards Jesus would be considered a lower class, poor man, maybe even a homeless vagabond with lapsed judgment. To His credit He would not be seen as a slick televangelist, but as an itinerant street preacher, aimlessly walking from place to place, attracting sinners, common folks, and prostitutes (21:31-32). The church crowd would miss Jesus because He would hang out where saints don't go. You would find Jesus at the local bars, clubs, and pubs ministering to the drunks. As a result of His association with alcoholics, He would be called a drunkard by the condemning, finger pointing church crowd stationed across the street inside their plush, pristine basilicas (Matthew 11:19). The great thing about Jesus is that He never let the press clippings or the court of public opinion alter His passion, His Person, or His purpose.

Jesus lived off the donations of others (Luke 8:1-3) and He fed people spiritually with the Word of God (Matthew 4:4, Luke 5:3, John 6:45). As a result His disciples made sure He was fed physically under the principles of the Old Testament (Deuteronomy 25:4, I Corinthians 9:7-9). The poor were not forgotten because Jesus regularly addressed poverty in His sermons (Matthew 5:1-6, 23:14), conversations (Matthew 19:21) and His parables (Matthew 25:31-46). Whenever He reached out to heal the blind, the crippled, and the diseased, He was reaching out to heal the poor and slighted in that culture. These were the ones He would go on to feed physical food (Matthew 14:13-21, Mark 8:1-10). On two separate occasions the Bible reveals that Jesus fed the multitudes by the thousands (Matthew 14:13-21, 15:32-39).

If you notice, Jesus never interviewed or qualified the people He fed to see if they were deserving of His charity. They didn't fill out applications or place their names in His data bank for "follow up". They were hungry so He simply fed them with no strings attached. Jesus didn't exploit the poor nor did He see feeding the hungry as a chance to pose for a picture with them for His next support letter or television show. In fact, in John's portrayal of the feeding of the 5,000 Jesus only preached to the people when they sought Him out the next day on the other side of the Sea of Galilee (John 6:22-26). He didn't preach while they were hungry because He knew it would be hard to hear about a good God when your stomach was growling.

On the very next day the people Jesus fed expected Him to take care of them again, possibly revealing a sense of entitlement. That's our greatest challenge in helping the hurting—how do we empower people without enabling them? How do we supply resources to the poor while simultaneously teaching them to rely upon God as their ultimate source? The people Jesus fed were looking for breakfast but He introduced them to *the Bread that came down from heaven* (John 6:41). They didn't expect that. Jesus went from offering physical bread to offering the spiritual bread of Himself, and unfortunately the people rejected Him. They only wanted what they could get from Him.

Jesus may have been meek but He definitely wasn't weak. He called them on their impure motives.

Like Jesus, we should feed hungry people in our reach without qualifying them. We must earn the right to be heard before offering Jesus to them. Also, we shouldn't get discouraged or take it personal if they reject our Savior. We shouldn't be overly surprised if the people we feed and minister to only want our goods but not our God. In the words of Earth, Wind, and Fire, "That's the way of the world." Jesus didn't let their rejection stop Him and it shouldn't stop us. However, we need to be wise as serpents (Matthew 10:16) and bold enough to lovingly confront user mentalities in the people we serve. This is especially true when compassionate white Christians serve among poor, ethnic minorities.

On several occasions I have witnessed how poor blacks have guilt tripped and manipulated whites to be their Christian cash cows and sanctified Santa Clauses. That's why it's best for whites to go into the communities with other ethnic minorities or partnered up with local churches or urban ministries already on the ground in the neighborhoods. We must realize that many poor people are brilliant at playing on people's emotions and hustling those with very little street smarts. Being a Christian doesn't mean that you should be a sucker. On some occasions we should give away our cloaks when asked and turn the other cheek when mistreated (Matthew 5:38-42). Sometimes we have to be like Jesus and know when to rise up, shake the dust off, and move to other cities and people when we sense embedded attitudes of entitlement, disrespect, and calloused unbelief (Matthew 10:14). Thank God for the Holy Spirit because He promised to lead us (Romans 8:14) and supply us with wisdom in those times (James 1:5), but keep in mind that if and when a poor person rips you off, at least your heart will be in the right place and great is your reward.

THE POOR ARE FOR SURE

The Bible records a story where Jesus made a profound statement about the poor after a lady anointed Him with costly oil before His death. It reads, *"And being in Bethany at the house of a leper, as He sat at the table, a woman came having an alabaster flask of costly oil of spikenard. Then she broke the flask and poured it on His head. But there were some who were indignant among themselves, and said, 'Why was this fragrant oil wasted? For it might have been sold for more than three hundred denarii and given to the poor.' And they criticized her sharply. But Jesus said, 'Let her alone. Why do you trouble her? She has done a good work for Me. For you have the poor with you always, and whenever you wish you may do them good; but Me you do not have always"* (Mark 14:3-7).

Jesus said that poor people will always be a part of society and He didn't seem pressed to change their status. He loosely quoted Moses from Deuteronomy 15:11 that says, *"For the poor will never cease from the land; therefore I command you, saying, 'You shall open your hand wide to your brother, to your poor and your needy in the land.'"* The only people I know who have a problem with what Jesus and Moses said are today's prosperity preachers. They cannot have a financially poor Savior or One that endorses perpetual poverty because that would violate and contradict the entire premise of their faulty theology. Not only must Jesus be rich in their estimation, but poverty is also a curse in their dollar signed eyes. If Jesus says that poor people will be an ongoing aspect of society, then that means He acknowledges the reality of poverty and the existence thereof. The world needs poor people because when we serve and touch them, God lets us in on what His heart is like. God's best treasures to mankind are often wrapped in plain, unpretentious people. Christians usually miss out on the best lessons in life because we keep walking by the ordinary so as to unwrap and cherish the extravagant. A lot of these finer gifts may look good on the outside, but they often end up lacking depth on the inside.

Poverty doesn't throw God for a loop the way it does some of us. In the Diverse Kingdom, there are worse things than being poor. Being financially rich and spiritually lost is worse than being poor. Jesus used this concept in a parable He told concerning a rich man and a crippled beggar named Lazarus (Luke 16:19-31). We must see that Jesus gave a specific name to the poor man but He did no such thing for the rich man. Whenever you remember someone's name or call a person by their name you are giving them honor and respect. It shows that they are cared for, valued and appreciated. Jesus brought dignity to the poor in this simple yet profound way.

Like God knows the names of the billions of stars in the heavens (Psalm 147:4), so God knows the poor by name even though the world doesn't. Our society often sees the poor as massive irritants and headaches. We need God's eyes because He sees the last as first (Matthew 19:30). In this parable Jesus compared the quality of life and its circumstances between the rich man and Lazarus in the light of eternity. By the time Jesus finishes speaking there appears to be no rational comparison (Luke 16:25). Jesus leaves the listener to make a choice, "Would I rather be like poor, crippled Lazarus or the rich man? Eternally speaking what's better, to be rich and healthy now and go to hell forever when I die, or to be crippled now and be made healthy later in glory with God?" Lazarus, the hero of Jesus' message, went to Abraham's bosom, also known as Paradise (Luke 23:43, II Corinthians 12:1-4), while the rich man opened his eyes in Hades (Luke 16:23), which was also known as Prison (I Peter 3:19). Jesus said that the poor, crippled Lazarus received *"evil things"* in this life but he was obviously blessed in the life to come (Luke 16:25).

RICH SAINT, POOR SAINT

You really don't have a diverse church without poor people active in attendance, leadership, or officially a part of the membership. And if they are there they shouldn't be exploited or mistreated (James 2:1-6). When our hearts and efforts do not bend toward the hurting, the poor, and the devastated, it can be questioned if our hearts are truly bent towards Jesus Christ. The Bible says, *"The righteous care about justice for the poor"* (Proverbs 29:7). The Lord's half- brother James said, *"Pure and undefiled religion before God and the Father is this: to visit orphans and widows in their trouble, and to keep oneself unspotted from the world"* (James 1:27).

Remember when Paul received the right hand of fellowship from the church leaders in Jerusalem? In that moment they challenged him to remember the poor (Galatians 2:9-10). Paul said that wouldn't be a problem for him because that's what he was eager to do. He practiced what he preached because many years later while stationed in Antioch, Paul oversaw an economic mission to help the poor believers in Jerusalem (Acts 11:27-30). The people who asked Paul to remember the poor ended up being the poor and Paul remembered them and helped them. Paul had been poor himself (II Corinthians 6:10). He worked with his hands as a tent maker (Acts 18:3) and didn't demand pay from the people he ministered to even though he could have as an apostle (I Corinthians 9:1-18). He learned to be content in poverty and he knew how to receive gifts when people blessed him (Philippians 4:10-19).

The Bible says, *"Better is the poor who walks in integrity than one perverse in his ways, though he may be rich"* (Proverbs 28:6). Proverbs 29:13 says, *"The poor man and the oppressor have this in common: The LORD gives light to the eyes of both."* Proverbs 22:2 says, *"The rich and the poor have this in common, the LORD is the maker of them all."* This means that God makes some people poor and others rich, therefore poverty cannot be a sin or a curse anymore than wealth is a sin or a curse. Both states are temporal, earthly classifications. Poor people aren't always poor because they are irresponsible or lazy, and rich people aren't always rich because they are responsible or hardworking. God decides who will have how much, and it appears that He gives the advantage to the poor. James 1:9 says that the lowly brother has an exalted position over the rich. Why is that? The answer may be found in James 2:5 that reads, *"Listen my beloved brethren: Has God not chosen the poor of this world to be rich in faith and heirs of the kingdom which He promised to those who love Him?"*

Poor people are usually richer in faith than rich people. Poor people usually have an advantage in the "living by faith" department because they have truly learned how to depend on and wait on God, whereas the well off and the wealthy are rarely put to the test this way. When a poor person testifies about God's miraculous power to provide it has more substance to it than when a rich person shares. Most of us can write a check or make a phone call to get some help, but the poor don't have access to these kinds of resources. Whenever I go to poor communities or countries and serve among the poor I am always put to shame by my lack of faith. People who have far less than I do materially usually have far more than I have by way of faith in God. When poor saints sing to God it seems to trump my praise, but somehow in the context of diverse community we encourage one another. This is where equality comes in. II Corinthians 8:14 in the NIV says, *"At the present time your plenty will supply what they need, so that in turn their plenty will supply what you need. Then there will be equality."*

Have you ever thought of poor people having a kind of plenty that wealthy people need? Equality comes when the rich and the poor mutually empower one another. I obviously need what the poor has by way of faith, and evidently the poor needs something I have by way of material resources. The Bible says when we give to the poor we lend to the Lord (Proverbs 19:17). In God's economic stimulus plan, He always pays back with interest when we give to His causes with the right motives. God gives to us so that we might keep on giving, especially to the poor. We need the poor more than they need us because we receive more from the poor than we can ever give to them. A sweater or a car that we give to the less fortunate will eventually wear out and break down. However, that feeling in our hearts and that change in our thinking as a result of interacting with the social outcasts of society stick with us for life. The poor inside and outside of our churches keep us grounded, humble, sensitive, and in tune with the heart of God. The rich and the not so rich are to comprise the local church's makeup (Acts 2:45, 4:32-37). We are to partner together as one team in outreach endeavors as well (II Corinthians 8:16-24).

In our church, you will never know whom the wealthy and the poor happen to be. We all rub shoulders together. We all serve and give together. There's no segregated seating or preferential treatment that you find in James 2:1-4.

Sometimes our rich people will dress down and our poorer members will dress up (Proverbs 13:7). We don't make any mention out of what people make, wear, drive, or where they live. Like Paul teaches us in Philippians 4:10-13, we are learning to be content with such things that we have, whether we are abounding or suffering need.

FINAL THOUGHT

The poor will always be here and Jesus expects us to do good to them and by them. Helping the poor doesn't always mean giving them money. It may mean training and offering them a job, giving them dignity by respecting them, looking them in the eye when you talk to them, shaking their hand, hugging and touching them, eating their food, visiting their home, and giving them a pleasant greeting by name. It may mean taking them in to your home periodically, giving them a ride or some sort of material blessing like a coat, a pair of shoes, a car, or an umbrella.

When my older brother Harold relocated from Baltimore to Tennessee a few years ago there were people in our church that stepped up to help him until he could get on his feet to help himself. They took him shopping and helped furnish his apartment. Because my brother had a prison record, we knew it would be difficult for him to find a meaningful, well paying job, but that's when one of God's people stepped up, remembered the poor, and offered my brother a job in his company. My brother and his lovely wife Brenda are doing great. This man who once lived on the street being addicted to drugs is now one of my deacons and has even enrolled back into college.

In the Jewish economy they were told when gleaning their fields to leave the edges non-harvested for the poor to come and help themselves (Leviticus 19:9-10). This was the kindness that Boaz afforded Ruth (Ruth 2:1-8). He empowered her and then she later empowered him as his wife (Ruth 4:13) and all of us by being in the lineage of the Messiah (Matthew 1:5). God made provision in the Law for this to happen. This gave people a hand up without just giving them a hand out per se. The have's will always exist and so will the have not's. God wants it to be that the have's would give to the have not's so that everyone can be the have some's.

2. THE POLITICS OF THE BLOODS AND THE CRIPS

Our southern city of Franklin, Tennessee is a historic, conservative, majority white, and politically "red" community situated in the buckle of the Bible belt. Franklin sits inside of Williamson County and has for the longest time been one of the wealthiest counties in the entire state of Tennessee. Even though it can be pretty alienating at times, I love it here. I know without a doubt God called me to raise my kids and minister in Williamson County. Being here for almost 20 years, I liken our red city to South Central Los Angeles in the 80's and 90's when street gangs were at an apex, terrorizing various communities with violence, drug trafficking, and prostitution.

The rival street gangs "The Bloods" and "The Crips" are still major forces today in many cities across the United States and they identify themselves and their territories by the colors they wear. Like the Republican Party, the Bloods wear red hats and sweatshirts, and like the Democratic Party, the Crips wear blue bandanas and shirts. If a person naively wore red clothes in a blue neighborhood or blue clothes in a red neighborhood they could find themselves in a world of trouble and possible bodily harm. Even non-gang members and innocent bystanders are mindful of the established color code and do not wear the opposing gang's colors in the wrong neighborhoods.

Politically speaking, I'm neither red nor blue but it's obvious that I'm in a red city. As a result, I always have to look over my shoulder during an election year if I should ever decide to go against the overall political climate and vote blue. I'm sure other people feel the same way if they live in a blue neighborhood and they decide to vote red. I understand that political partisanship is to occur because that is how our democracy works, but I'm not sure if there is a place for bullying tactics and partisan politics in our churches. It grieves me when churches fall in line with partisan politics and become known as red churches or blue congregations. Although these churches and ministers say "the politically correct thing" that they are non-partisan, it is clear where they stand if you listen long enough to the pastors preach. In these supposedly impartial institutions you can find yourself being blasted, belittled, and ousted if you don't subscribe to the church's particular political color. Voting leaflets left behind in the foyer are dead giveaways concerning the church's political slants and biases.

What's interesting in my community is that just down the road, our neighboring county Davidson is blue. Davidson County which is more economically and ethnically diverse than Williamson County, houses the blue city of Nashville. And even though my city is a red "Bloods" territory politically, my church is both blue and red in its make up, mindset, and membership. To my knowledge I was the only pastor in our city that had this dubious challenge during the recent presidential debates, election, and Barack Obama's historic inauguration. The churches in my town are primarily one-dimensional politically, economically, and ethnically. Our church is 44% African American and 43% Caucasian. The remaining 13% is comprised of Hispanics, Native Americans, Africans, and Asians, and these all have varying political affiliations. We have black republicans and white democrats in our church.

It's easy to preach to the choir if your choir is all Democrat or all Republican. It's easy to get "Amen's" from the congregation if your church is homogenous and votes the same way all the time, but how do you preach to the people and get "Amen's" if your assembly is comprised of both "Bloods and Crips"? Remember, gang members are a highly territorial brood of vipers. One misplaced word or ill-placed sentence could lead to a gang fight in the pews of God's house or fatal, verbal drive bys in the parking lot after church. I know what the easy, spiritual answer is. Some have said, "Pastor Chris, just preach the Word of God and let God move on people's hearts for His will and for His glory." I wish it were that easy. In our city that kind of wisdom often means, "Just preach the Word of God because everyone knows God is more in line with the Republicans than He is with the Democrats."

Nothing is more potentially divisive among evangelical Christians than to discuss politics, race, and religion. In President Obama you have all three points of possible contention and I'm not sure we really want to go there openly, honestly, and humbly as evangelical Christians. By now everyone knows the statistics that the vast majority of African Americans usually and unquestionably vote democratic and the vast majority of white evangelicals usually and unquestionably vote republican. But where do people like me go who are African American but not democrat, and who are evangelical but not republican? Think about that. Obama's rise had many black evangelicals pondering and digging for plausible support. We had never seen anything like him before. He was not like Jesse Jackson. Obama was not like Allen Keys. He was something totally different. We liked him as a person but as evangelical Christians we didn't like some of his politics.

THE BEAUTY IS IN THE BALANCE

God rescued me from that deserted island of evangelical arrogance and now I'm somewhere in "no man's land". There aren't any rulebooks here or catchy slogans to hide behind. You have to think and ponder over both sides well, eating the chicken and throwing out the bones from both. I have now discovered that I am too conservative for the liberals and too liberal for the conservatives. I'm somewhere in the middle, somewhere in the gray, and that's just not with politics either. In the words of my friend Kirk Whalum, "I am learning to listen with my left ear as well as my right ear." No wonder James, the Lord's brother said, *"So then, my beloved brethren, let every man be quick to listen, so to speak, slow to wrath;"* (James 1:19). God gave us two ears and one mouth for a reason, huh?

I have been blessed to the degree that I can hear Martin and I can hear Malcolm. I can hear the positive and negative points of a republican and I can hear the positive and negative points of a democrat. I enjoy listening to Stevie Wonder and I love listening to Steven Curtis Chapman. I read James Dobson and I read Jim Wallis. I'm in the middle, and therefore I'm too black for some whites and not black enough for some blacks. I understand a little bit how Dr. King must have felt as he tried to bring typically opposing sides together. You catch it from both sides and when arrows come from all directions only God can be your shield (Psalm 84:11). Some Christians see the middle road as the highway of compromise. Maybe it is for some but I truly like it in the middle because the beauty and the tension are in the balance. We grow best in the balance. We need God's Spirit and wisdom to teach us how to compromise without compromising.

I am a Christian, who is black by providential design. I live by evangelical Christian beliefs that primarily sprung forth from white, western Christian thinkers. I have a heart for social change among the poor, illiterate, under-served, underprivileged, and marginalized of our country. As an evangelical Christian, I believe in the inerrancy of Scripture, the virgin birth and deity of Jesus Christ, the atoning death and bodily resurrection of Jesus Christ, the necessity for all to know Jesus Christ as the only means of salvation, and the evangelizing of the world with this gospel. These are the beliefs that typically characterize an evangelical, but somewhere along the way the term "evangeli-cal" came to represent an unwavering political stance for the right.

Somehow the term "evangelical" became synonymous with white, middle to upper income, conservative Christians who have an agenda to regulate morality through legislation. This means that "liberals" and "non-believers" are all lumped together in a pile on the left, widening the chasm between the so-called enlightened and the unenlightened. Evangelicals now had their own cable news stations, books, and radio personalities who heralded their perspectives and dogged the left in the process. This made the left snap back and rebel many times to the extreme as a way to stoke the ire of the right. Somewhere along the line the word "republican" came to stand for "right" and the word "democrat" came to stand for "wrong", I mean "left". The truth is both parties need constant overhauls and adjustments because neither is perfect. As I stand in the middle, often alone, I have a decent view of this.

THE SOCIAL GOSPEL

I once had a discussion with a prominent, white Christian leader and the idea of the "social gospel" came up in our conversation. He emphatically told me that there was no place for a social gospel and anyone who thought that way was in error. He went on to tell me that he understood where I was coming from as a young, black man because he himself was part Cherokee Indian. He strongly declared that the Jewish Holocaust was more destructive in nature than the African slave trade. I responded by saying they were both terrible atrocities and I didn't see how he could place a value on one tragedy involving millions of human lives over the other. By the time our conversation was finished I was appalled by his ignorance but unfortunately not surprised.

There is such a premium put on saving the soul of a person that we often miss the whole of a person. Conservative evangelicals denounce the "social gospel" as if Jesus never ministered socially. When He fed the 5,000 in John chapter 6 He didn't have the multitudes sit through a sermon presentation before they could get a fish sandwich. He simply fed them with no strings attached and left. That's social ministry. Jesus didn't preach a sermon to them until the next day and that was only when the people came looking for Him in order to get breakfast (John 6:25-26). At this point Jesus rebuked them and they listened to Him declare the truth of God's Word. They still rejected Him, but at least He had taken a social interest in them and their empty stomachs. They knew He cared for them socially even though they disagreed and rejected Him spiritually as the eternal Bread of Life. Jesus earned the right to be heard even though the crowds didn't "hear" Him. Jesus, the ultimate balanced One, was Lamb and Lion, the Root and the Shoot of David, and He was equally God and Man. He led a wonderful, balanced, pragmatic ministry, never relying on cookie cutter programs or decision driven evangelism to reach people's souls only.

Like Jesus, I am concerned about people's health. I care about affordable healthcare for all Americans even if that means my personal plan may have to change some to help accommodate others. That's not too much to ask. In my opinion 75 million people without healthcare is a moral issue that should concern the church. I care about the 147 million orphans around the world that need families to adopt them. I care about human rights for the abortionist and the homosexual even though I disagree strongly with the sins of abortion and homosexuality. Somehow I have to witness to these people without condemning them. It's easier to sit across the street and judge the sinner and his sins than it is to walk across the street where the sinner dwells, understand their world and love them with the love and truth of God whether they immediately change or not. I believe Jesus did that (Luke 23:34).

DONKEYS OR ELEPHANTS?

For far too long evangelicals have given Jesus a less than admirable representation to the world. We have become too satisfied for the mainstream to know what we stand opposed to rather than to let them know what we stand for. I don't believe Jesus ministered this way among the lost. For instance, we know Jesus is against homosexual unions even though it can't be emphatically proven from a biblical perspective that He ever publicly denounced homosexuality in the four gospels. Some have taken His silence to mean acceptance, but we do know emphatically what Jesus stood for. Jesus was for monogamous, heterosexual marital unions because of what He publically proclaimed and stood for from a biblical perspective (Matthew 19:1-9).

No matter how noble the cause, Jesus Christ does not ride the backs of Democrat donkeys or Republican elephants. Jesus doesn't ride on men's bandwagons because bandwagons break down, become derailed, get side tracked, fluctuate, crash, phase out, and thrive on opinions. Since Jesus Christ doesn't ride man's bandwagons neither should His people. Whenever men take sides exclusively with and for other men, then childish rifts are not far behind. This party posturing happened in the church of Corinth as it pertained to baptism (I Corinthians 1:10-17). As Dr. Tony Evans likes to say, "God doesn't take sides. He takes over." Dr. Evans developed this thought from the passage of Scripture where Joshua met up with the Angel of the Lord prior to the Jews invasion of Jericho (Joshua 5:13-15). Joshua saw a Man that he didn't know or recognize dressed in battle array. Joshua wanted to know whose side was the Man on. We could assume that this Man, who is a pre-incarnate appearance of Jesus Christ in the Old Testament, would be on the side of Israel, but Jesus made it clear He wasn't on either side. As commander of the Lord's army it would behoove any and all to be on Jesus' side. That's what counts.

Many Christians assume Jesus is in line with Republicans because of their perceived intentions to defend life in the womb, fight for traditional marriage, support Israel, fight just wars against terrorism, and the encouragement of hard work and healthy capitalism for a better economy. Many Christians believe Jesus is in line with Democrats because of their perceived intentions to acknowledge and change the plight of the poor, help the sick and the elderly, lift up the lower and middle classes, holistically include and empower minorities, improve education, and to establish world peace without emphasizing the use of military force. But the question isn't: Is Jesus in line with Republicans or is He in line with Democrats? The true question is: Are Democrats and Republicans in line with Jesus?

The truth is both parties have "perceived intentions" that rarely manifest to actual, positive betterment for the American people. Both parties have traits that are both consistent and inconsistent with sound Biblical principles. Neither party fully represents the interests of God or the people of God. Christians always say that our trust is not in the government but in God and His church. It's time we started living like we really believe that.

QUESTIONS AND ANSWERS

1. What is the danger of conservative, evangelical Christians becoming so closely affiliated and identified with the Republican Party? As with being aligned with any party, you will find yourself having to explain or deny the corruption that is prevalent within the party. Close political association hinders our ability to reach all kinds of lost people who sit outside of our persuasion. At this point, the church becomes the caboose and not the engine (Matthew 5:13).

2. Is it possible to be a disciple of Jesus and be a Democrat or vote for a Democrat? Absolutely. Our church has Democrats and Republicans in it, and it's awesome that many of the Democrats are white and many of the Republicans are black. Perhaps if there were more theologically sound, ethically astute Christians in the Democratic Party there would be less potential for moral compromise. If there were more theologically sound, socially active Christians in the Republican Party there would be more attention given to matters of empowerment across the board.

3. Should a candidate's position on pro-life issues be the most important thing for Christians to consider before voting? For some Christians pro-life is the primary issue to consider when voting and that is totally understandable. Christians believe that life not only begins at conception, we believe that life begins before conception in the heart and plans of God (Jeremiah 1:5). The cry of innocent blood from abortions (and unjust wars) can bring about the wrath of God on the land (Genesis 4:10-11, 9:6), and Christians are called to speak up for those who cannot speak for themselves (Proverbs 31:8). However, one must consider that there are other "life issues" that stir the hearts of believers as well. Other Christians may have life issue concerns about gun control, health care, addressing and working against poverty, and ending wars to name a few (Proverbs 31:9).

Consider the biblical character Job. Job's quality of life was adversely affected when he went from having everything to losing everything (Job 1:1-21). This led Job to eventually lose his spiritual focus, curse the day of his birth, and wish he were dead (Job 3:1-5). Job even wondered why he had not been aborted in the womb (Job 3:11). This tells us that extreme poverty, poor health, and substandard living conditions have a way of making people wish they had been aborted. These issues bring misery (Proverbs 31:7). What good is fighting for life in the womb if lives outside of the womb wish they were dead due to poverty? Shouldn't we fight for life inside as well as outside of the womb? Is one life more valuable than the other in the heart of God? Yes, Christians should fight against the sin of abortion and we should fight against the severe conditions of life that make grown people wish they had been aborted.

4. Should a candidate's position on marriage be the most important thing for Christians to consider before voting? Protecting the sanctity of marriage between a man and a woman should always be a Christian's concern in these last days (I Timothy 4:1-6). Married Christians can help protect the sanctity of marriage by staying married! A lack of divorce proves that marriage works. Homosexual unions will never be blessed or sanctioned by the God of the Bible (Genesis 2:24, Hebrews 13:4). In addition, we should also ask ourselves when voting, why was Sodom and Gomorrah destroyed? It was not destroyed primarily because of homosexuality. It was also destroyed because they overlooked the poor. Ezekiel 16:49-50 says, *"Look, this was the* *iniquity of your sister Sodom: She and her daughter had pride, fullness of food, and abundance of idleness; neither did she strengthen the hand of the poor and needy. And they were haughty and committed abomination before Me; therefore I took them away as a I saw fit."*

5. Why do most African Americans tend to loyally and unquestionably vote Democratic? In the 1860s, blacks started off as loyalists to the Republican Party because of its founding by several anti-slavery groups. Also, Abraham Lincoln was a Republican and he was the man who "freed the slaves". One hundred years later, the political loyalty of blacks shifted to the Democratic Party when John F. Kennedy helped get Rev. Martin Luther King, Jr. out of a Birmingham jail in 1963. And then under Democrat Lyndon Johnson, the Civil Rights Act of 1964 and the Voting Rights Act of 1965 were passed giving blacks their greatest social strides as a people since emancipation. Ever since then the majority of Blacks have primarily aligned with, run for office as, and voted for Democrats.

6. Why do most white, conservative Christians tend to either ignore or inadequately address many social issues like poverty, crime, funding for inner city schools, affordable healthcare, unemployment, injustice, racial profiling, and affordable housing to name a few? This is unfamiliar territory for many white people because they usually don't have ongoing relationships with people who fit into these categories; therefore there is little chance for true compassion and sympathy to develop. Many conservative whites didn't grow up under substandard conditions so it's difficult and inconvenient to identify with the socially disadvantaged. Plus, if you have been told over and over that these people are where they are because they are lazy, irresponsible, and ignorant, you begin to believe it. If you feel that these people are the exclusive source for their own problems, then you will lack the sympathy and compassion to serve and lift them up.

7. Should a pastor influence or dictate to his church how to vote and who to vote for? Absolutely not, and this goes far beyond keeping the church's tax exemption status in check! If a pastor teaches the Bible holistically and with balance, the Holy Spirit will teach God's people how to vote. A pastor should never insult our intelligence or deny us the privilege as Americans to choose based on our convictions. We must bear in mind that God will hold all of us accountable for how we vote (Romans 14:12).

8. Is the country's wellbeing contingent upon Christians being elected and holding office? The United States government is not a Christian institution therefore it is not mandatory for Christians to be at the helm. We cannot assume that qualifications for political office are predominately spiritual. Would you prefer a Christian doctor or a pagan doctor? It all depends, right? A pagan may be the most experienced person in the particular field of medicine that affects you the most. Besides, Christians tend to vote for a political messiah rather than a solid political leader. No past or present government official who is a Christian has been the sole solution to a flawed government or a flawed society. If it were that simple I would qualify to be president of the U.S. because I love Jesus and I support Israel. I work hard, and I oppose abortion and homosexual marriage, so I guess I'm qualified to be the next President of the United States according to traditional evangelical standards.

9. What should a church's political affiliation be? A church should be non-partisan. When a church or a particular denomination is known more for its political posturing than it is for Jesus- watch out, "Ichabod" is on the way (I Samuel 4:21-22)! When the church inordinately lies down with politics it should not be surprised if it gets up with fleas of compromise. Could the current let down by the Republican Party cause Christians to become critical thinkers and look to God only for change? Could the shortcomings and liberality of the Democratic Party cause Christians to think Biblically and to reconsider their kingdom priorities if America is to change for the better?

10. Do you feel that African American Christians who voted for Barack Obama compromised their Christian integrity? I actually received this question from people who did not realize how shrouded it was in pompous, evangelical elitism. If one group of people has to answer to another group of people that has opposing views, then yes, they compromised by voting for Obama. But since individuals have to answer to God, who are we to judge another person's voting decisions (Romans 14:1-5)? Like every other president, Barack Obama is first a politician. He is not the Christ. I don't believe he is the Antichrist either. Like all of us, I pray he is a man who daily sees his need for Christ. Many blacks likely voted for Obama because they were strongly driven by the notion of having the nation's first black president. Is that concept entirely wrong from the vantage point of the historically oppressed? For some it may be wrong, whereas for others it is encouraging. Other Christians were drawn by the idealism of change presented by Obama's platform. Voting can be a highly complex and emotional matter. That's why Americans vote in private booths. You shouldn't have to vote the way I vote in order to be loved and received by me. We must realize that God doesn't lead Christians to vote the same way. However, He has called His church to work together as one once the voting booths are closed.

WHAT SHOULD WE DO AS CHRISTIANS?

Christians should pray for our political leaders whether we voted for them or not (I Timothy 2:1-3). We should submit to the governing authorities and pay our taxes (Romans 13:1-7). As United States citizens, Christians are expected to participate in the political process, whether by running for office, voting, or serving in local civic matters. We should practice being respectful dual citizens (Philippians 3:20), and personally vote our conscience and our convictions. We should practice listening openly and objectively to opposite views and perspectives, and although there are two primary parties we must remember there is only one America.

We should resist political arrogance and spiritual imbalance. We should resist compromising truth in the name of change, tolerance, and acceptance. We must recognize that each political party has its strengths and weaknesses, and our system is supposed to work best through checks and balances. Contrasts are meant to enhance and compliment, and not always bring about a sense of combat. We must operate like the local church is God's primary institution for change in the earth and not the government (Matthew 5:13-16, 16:18-19, Ephesians 1:22-23). We must understand that the government and its elected officials, whether Democrat, Independent, or Republican, are ordained by God (Romans 13:1-5), and when the dust settles we must be relieved by the fact that God is sovereign (Psalm 75:6-7), Jesus does and will reign (Isaiah 9:6-7), and all things will work out for His pleasure and purposes (Revelation 21:1-7)!

3. BRIDGING THE DENOMINATIONAL DIVIDE

God has a sense of humor. He has to have one because He works with me. I came to Nashville, Tennessee in 1992 for the sole purpose of furthering my music career in gospel rap. Our group Transformation Crusade was on the Benson Record label and we made two CD's while still being students in college and seminary in Lynchburg, Virginia. Once all of the members of the group graduated, we moved to Nashville to pursue full-time music ministry with great expectations of going to the next level, whatever that was.

It seemed like once I unloaded the last box from the U-Haul truck and carried it into my Nashville apartment that the record company called and said they were not going to make another CD with our group. I couldn't believe it! We had been dropped because we didn't sell enough units. I immediately cried out to God, or should I say, whined up to God, and said, "Why did you bring me all the way to Nashville to let this happen? You could have prevented this or You could have left me in Virginia or sent me back home to Maryland!" I was hot with anger and boiling with resentment. I would have never come to Nashville on my own accord so I was upset that God would lead me there and pull the carpet out from under my feet once I arrived.

Being a newlywed I had to find a job. You can't live on love for long so I began working in a metal shop just up the road in Franklin, Tennessee and I hated it. Every morning I wondered why God allowed me to go through all of this. Here I was called to the ministry, ordained, trained, and possessing a Master's degree and I was working in a metal shop fixing locks and pipes for a display company.

MIXING IT UP WITH PRESBYTERIANS

After six months at the metal shop things began to change. My good friend and former Transformation Crusade band mate, Andre Sims, was approached by a large white congregation in Franklin, Tennessee called Christ Community Church. They were a part of the Presbyterian Church in America (PCA) denomination and they placed great emphasis on the tenets of reformed theology and the practical outworking of God's grace. They wanted to see if Andre would consider coming on staff with them because they needed a black male to help bolster and legitimize their outreach into the black communities that were not far from the church's downtown campus. Because of a previous commitment at another church, Andre declined their offer and suggested they talk with me about the job.

Here's God sense of humor again. He was about to pair up a black, rap music loving, Baptist trained, soul food eating brother with a bunch of white, wealthy, reformed, middle-aged, acoustic guitar worshipping Presbyterians! Can't you hear God laughing? My Armenian arguments were about to collide with their Calvinistic conclusions. My premillennial views of Christ's return were on a crash course with their views of Amillennialism. My legalism was about to be confronted by their freedom in Christ, and my works-based, performance-driven approach to Christianity was about to be dwarfed by their transforming message of grace and spiritual adoption. Of all the places God could have placed me He chose to place me there. Didn't God remember that I was tired of being the lone black guy in all white settings? Didn't God remember that He was the One that placed me in a Baptist family and sent me to a Baptist university and seminary? Why was He leading me to mix things up now with these Presbyterians? I soon discovered that God has to mix things up in our lives in order to straighten us out.

When my wife Dorena and I came to Christ Community Church in January of 1993 the music and style of worship were different and simpler. Nevertheless it was still very penetrating. The preaching was calmer than what I was used to, but it was definitely solid. I was used to getting heat from black preachers that I loved, but the white preachers brought the light in their delivery. Both are needed but rarely combined. I would eventually learn how to preach with both heat and light, being informative and passionate. Although there was never a formal "altar call" given during the service, I felt myself responding to God every Sunday in a fresh, heartfelt way.

I was interviewed, hired, and brought on staff as a pastoral intern to work with a ministry of the church called Franklin Community Ministries (FCM).

81

A fiery red-haired lady named Paige Overton (Pitts) lead FCM and I learned so much from her about doing ministry and serving the poor. I had never been under a woman before and through this, God began to heal me from ecclesiastical chauvinism. Not once did my new brothers in the Lord demand that I become ordained in the PCA. Not once did they say I had to accept their doctrinal positions before working there on staff. Our common ground was our belief in Jesus Christ as the Son of God and only resurrected Savior of the world. That was the main thing and they kept it the main thing. I had never witnessed this kind of willingness from a church to compromise without compromising. Secondary issues remained secondary, and as my heart began to open, my eyes opened as well.

Christ Community Church operated by a plurality of elders whereas I came from monarchial kinds of ministries. They taught grace giving and I devoutly believed in tithing. As a sign of the new covenant they baptized infants of covenant parents and I believed in believer's baptism by immersion. They drank alcohol and I didn't believe any Christian should ever imbibe of the grapes! They wore jeans and sandals to church and I wore my suits and dress shoes. They read from the New International Version (NIV) of the Bible and I was reared in the King James Version (KJV) of the Holy Scriptures. The KJV was good enough for Moses so it was good enough for me!

God must have been chuckling in heaven as I clumsily meandered through two years of discovering that the kingdom of God was a lot bigger than my experiences and perspectives. My ministerial and theological arrogances were a thin house of cards, and thankfully a wind from the Holy Spirit was on the way. I was on a constant learning curve that I first resisted but then slowly began to embrace. I soon found myself laughing at myself. Among these folks I saw love in word and deed that shattered my prejudices and extinguished my fears. As far as my outreach ministry was concerned, they got behind me and stood with me every step of the way. One of the church's pastors, Scott Roley, took me under his wing. When I first met Scott I questioned how well he knew the Lord because I judged him through my narrow, self-righteous eyes. He didn't act or look like any preachers I had ever known, and talk about transparency, Scott was quick to openly confess his sins to me due to his dependence upon the all-sufficient grace of God. I never heard a pastor be so honest. The stuff Scott confessed to me was the junk I struggled with but didn't have the courage to admit to anyone. I had a religious persona that hadn't yet cracked. Nevertheless, Scott showed me Jesus in a way that I had never seen him before. I was slowly getting freed up.

FCM held regular prayer meetings at Paige's house, and Scott and his wife Linda would attend along with Stu and Peggy Southard, and several other couples and individuals. We would earnestly pray for black kids by name and sing worship songs to a folk guitar played by Scott. These white lovers of Jesus blew me away! I soon realized that it was this group's prayers for a black man to join them in the ministry that caused me to lose my record contract. It seemed like they loved black people more than I did because they made personal sacrifices to reach them that I wasn't even willing to make. On top of all of this, the pastors of Christ Community Church allowed me to preach occasionally on Sunday mornings. That was a major gesture because it was the ultimate sign of acceptance to entrust me with that kind of authority and responsibility. After I preached, white people would come up to me and say, "If you ever start a church, please let us know." I had no clue what God was up to, but I knew He was up to something.

NIGHTMARE ON NATCHEZ STREET

The Bible says that Jesus went to His own people but they did not receive Him (John 1:12). I got a little taste of that myself because everyone in the city of Franklin didn't see God's hand in placing me with the large, white church in Franklin. The black ministers didn't initially embrace me and they assumed I was an Uncle Tom kind of brother. The pastor with the most influence in the black community at the time was a man named Reverend R.L. Denson. He was the pastor of the all black First Missionary Baptist Church on the corner of Ninth and Natchez Street. Reverend Denson was a stern, pro-black kind of man who came to Franklin, Tennessee from the south side of Chicago in the early 1990s. He didn't trust white people or black people who trusted white people. Reverend Denson was fine living his life not having to come into too much contact with white folks. In his younger years in Chicago, Denson was an advocate for the Black Panther Party and that extreme exposure impacted his perspective of ministry.

In time I had heard how Reverend Denson and Reverend Scott weren't seeing eye-to-eye in our beloved city. The two men had never met face to face but they had heard of one another. Christ Community was active in our "Jerusalem" by reaching out primarily to minority children and teenagers. They were sincere but sincerely wrong because the church never coordinated or even submitted their efforts to the gatekeepers in the black community of which Reverend Denson was chief. Unfortunately I followed in this misstep also. This would be a naive and costly mistake that further widened the chasm between the two churches.

Reverend Denson and many of the black church leaders viewed Christ Community Church's outreach ministry as arrogant, insensitive, typical, and cowardly because they focused primarily on getting to know children and teenagers and not the adults. When I came on staff with the church, I was considered the token black guy that the big, white church hired and brought in for window dressing. This caused Reverend Denson and I to be adversaries from the start. In my first encounter with him he lived up to his reputation. Paige and I went to Reverend Denson's church to invite him and his congregation to a concert that we were hosting with the black, contemporary Christian music group Anointed. Reverend Denson met us at the door and we never got invited inside the church, so we stood out front on the porch offering him and his church free tickets to the concert. Without cursing us out he politely and sternly told us what we could do with those tickets.

Looking back now, I realize my mistake. I tried to foster a relationship with a man through an event. That never works when there is underlying hostility and suspicion already present in the air. Our gesture looked like a bribe to Pastor Denson. That tactic may have worked with the kids in the community but it didn't work with him. Instead I should have asked to sit down and talk with him man to man so I could hear his heart and maybe he could have heard mine. If nothing else we could have possibly gained an understanding.

Unfortunately, whenever I rode through the Natchez neighborhood for the next two years in the blue church van to pick up kids for Good News Club, summer camp, and winter camp, weekly Bible study, and after school tutoring, I always kept my eyes open for Reverend Denson. I tried to avoid him like the plague, but he was one of those pastors that liked to walk the streets regularly, so I saw him all of the time. I would never stop and get out of my van to speak with him. Quite honestly, he intimidated me. I didn't understand how someone could say they loved Jesus and be blinded with such rage. But at the same time I too was blinded with racial naivety and ministry youthfulness. Even still, Reverend Denson didn't want us in the neighborhood, but I kept coming anyway. I had to ride by his church every time I came into the "hood" to pick up kids in his neighborhood and take them back to our church to minister to them. Reverend Denson would sharply say that when those same kids got sick, went to jail, or had trouble at home, it would be his church that would get the first phone call and not Christ Community Church. In other words, we were doing "ministry" but we weren't viewed as being a part of the true community on Natchez Street. His point was valid.

PLANTING GOD'S CHURCH AND NOT MY CHURCH

After a while I began to feel God speaking to my heart about planting a church. I had worked in the black neighborhoods for two years and I was deeply burdened for the breakdown of the African American family. I had been taught that God's church was the best way to break this cycle of disparity because the local church was the only way we could access and utilize the keys of the kingdom to unlock the gates of hell that were plaguing our city. The local church, like no other institution, provided the structure and stability of a surrogate family to the fatherless, widows, and orphans. So I decided to do what I said I would never do and that was to plant a church.

I assumed the church was going to be a black church, but God quickly reminded me that I needed to plant His church and not my church. I saw God at work giving me favor with people from both the black and white communities. I reread the book of Acts and multiculturalism jumped off the pages at me. I followed God's lead and began praying with people who were interested in planting a church that looked like the church in Antioch. To my surprise God led different kinds of people to me, two by two, like my name was Noah.

NO STRINGS ATTACHED

When I shared with the leaders of Christ Community Church that I was being called by God to start a multi-ethnic church they treated me like my name was Nehemiah. As you recall Nehemiah was burdened to rebuild the walls around the city of Jerusalem for his people just coming out of captivity to Babylon. God gave Nehemiah so much favor with King Xerxes of Persia that he decided to finance Nehemiah's mission to rebuild. Nehemiah was given lumber, an armed escort, and everything he needed to succeed (Nehemiah 1-3).

God seemed to give me that same kind of favor with my brothers and sisters of Christ Community Church to the degree that they offered me financial assistance without me asking for it. They decided to pay my salary in full for the first year of the church plant. They also offered to give me half my salary the second year and a third of my salary the third year. They said they would back their support off as my church became more and more self-sustaining. That was unheard of. I didn't have to join their denomination to get financial support from them. I didn't have to say publicly or in print that they helped plant the church. I wasn't told that they had to "oversee" everything our church did or have their hands in our affairs. They didn't ask for the money back or a percentage of our annual income. They offered the money to us with no strings attached whatsoever. Tell me if you see this happening everyday.

BUILDING BLOCKS FOR THE DEVIL

As I held prayer meetings in the summer months of 1995 with anyone interested in joining up with me, I was blessed to see black and white people come out to the prayer times in the prayer chapel of Christ Community Church. There were people coming from various Baptist persuasions, Presbyterian, Church of Christ, Charismatic, and un-churched backgrounds. Our church would be diverse by providential design and not by human manipulation.

I even decided to try visiting another black pastor in the neighborhood since Rev. Denson and I weren't on the same page. When I told the pastor my vision for planting a multi-ethnic church he told me, "Son, what you think you're building for God may end up being building blocks for the devil." Instead of dressing his comments up with religious garb he should have plainly said that "race mixing" was not allowed in church. He tried to discourage me from planting the church that God was building but it didn't work. I left there all the more committed to the vision and I decided I would never come back to him for wisdom. I shook the dust off.

After the summer prayer meetings, Strong Tower Bible Church was launched on September 3, 1995 and we held our first service in the aerobics room of the Franklin YMCA. I had about 30 people on the core team. I had very little idea what I was doing and that would prove to be a good thing. God blessed us tremendously and we had many wonderful times in worship and service. As the church grew in size I noticed that our membership was largely Caucasian by the tune of 80%. Our music was a sometimes a source of contention because it was imbalanced, sounding too contemporary. Contemporary singer Natalie Grant was our church secretary and she decided to form a choir. That was the turning point to balancing out our musical flavor because that little white girl was blessed with soul down deep.

Natalie, my wife, David and Nicole Mullen, and Todd and Nicol Smith of Selah began to infuse gospel into our worship services to accompany our contemporary style. We began to discover that musical style was secondary to musical intent and content. Intent is the heart or spirit of our worship and content is the truth. The Bible says that God is looking for people to worship Him with Spirit and truth (John 4:24) and I wanted Him to find the people of Strong Tower Bible Church fitting that description. I had to teach the people that the intent of the worshipper was crucial because a hungry soul shouldn't complain about the type of food set before him or her especially since God Himself was our Bread. Over time we developed a team of musicians and singers that would respect the various genres and musical expressions to the point that when they played and sang the music, they did so authentically and excellently. Plus it didn't hurt having jazz saxophonist Kirk Whalum join us and become our elder of worship. The more we stayed teachable and flexible, the more God kept providing.

HEALING IN A HOSPITAL PARKING LOT

I had made up my mind that I didn't need Reverend Denson, but God knew that I needed him. Even though God was graciously blessing my new church there was more He wanted for me. As faith would have it, one afternoon I went to the hospital to visit one of our members who was sick. Reverend Denson was there at the same time checking on one of his members. Both of us were in a tender place that day. We talked in the hospital parking lot and I noticed his heart had changed towards me. Something had happened to him. I found out later that Reverend Denson's heart changed as a result of participating in an ongoing prayer meeting (B1 Vitamin- Be Prayerful) with a black mentor and a white pastor of another denomination. At the same time I was part of a prayer meeting with Pastor Scott and a black pastor in the city named Hewitt Sawyers. We would cry out for harmony in our city and God decided this day to begin answering our prayers.

Reverend Denson was no longer criticizing me for being associated with a white church or for having white people in my church. He even apologized to me for how he had been harsh with me when I came to him years ago to promote the concert. I forgave him. I then apologized to him for not getting to know him before I rummaged through his neighborhood doing ministry. He forgave me. I finally found that acceptance from him that I always longed for but didn't want to admit. He was my elder and I needed his covering and blessing if God was going to bless my ministry in the city the way I wanted Him to. That day we experienced what the psalmist meant when he said, *"How good and pleasant it is when brothers dwell together in unity"* (Psalm 133:1).

There is no feeling like unity. There is no blessing of peace like forgiveness between two men who were too scared and too stubborn to reach towards one another but God chose to put us together in the right place at the right time. We were both broken men, and from that moment forth we knew we had been healed in that hospital parking lot. We came there to visit sick people and God ended up visiting us in our sickness. What glorious irony.

DENNY AND SCOTT

Not long after our coming together, Reverend Denson and Pastor Scott would finally get together. Scott walked into First Missionary Baptist Church to humble himself before Denny and apologize for not getting to know him even though their churches were around the corner from each other. As Pastor Scott came down the aisle, Reverend Denson was facing the altar and his back was towards Scott. Reverend Denson and Scott had never met face to face, but when he turned around and saw this white man standing in his church he knew it was Scott. The two men embraced and wept right in the middle of the aisle, confessing and apologizing to one another. Only God could do that. When news had come to me of their reconciliation I was on cloud nine! Two of my spiritual fathers, one black and one white, were now united and their friendship would change both of their lives and our city for the better. Something broke in the heavenly realms that day and God poured out a blessing that we didn't expect to receive. In the same city that the Methodist minister E.M. Bounds once prayed for revival during the Civil War, another war between brothers came to an end. In 1997, Scott and Denny, along with a host of other pastors and laymen from various churches and denominations founded the Empty Hands Fellowship, a non-denominational group of believers committed to fellowshipping with one another beyond racial and denominational boundaries. To this day Empty Hands Fellowship still meets and it has given birth to a ministry for pastors in our city called Synago. Synago is from the Greek word "synagogue" which means, "to come together". More and more pastors in our city and county have decided to come together in monthly prayer, fellowship, and acts of combined community service.

TO AFRICA AND BEYOND

In the years that would follow, Denny invited me to speak at his church on a number of occasions. He came and spoke at my church as well. He spoke at Christ Community Church and Scott preached at his church. In 1998 Rev. Denson, Scott, myself, and several members of the Empty Hands Fellowship traveled together to Benin, West Africa. We got to take part in a venture where the President of Benin, Matthew Kerikou, issued a formal apology to African Americans for his country's involvement in the slave trade. In addition to dining in the palace with the President and meeting one hundred kings of West Africa, we also took a guided tour to learn the systematic methods used by Africans and Europeans in the slave trade. We prayed together at the whipping tree. We were horrified at the House of Darkness, and we wept together on the shores where the slave ships once docked in order to load up its human cargo and leave for the Americas. We came home stirred all the more to keep building bridges across the denominational divide.

Denny and Scott were our leaders. They lived out reconciliation right before our eyes. They would sometimes travel the country and tell their story and speak on their friendship. Scott had relocated his family into a historically black, underserved neighborhood in our city and Denny kept his crusade of loving white people going on. Denny's world had changed and so did our city. He testified before Congress and twice met with President Bush and Condoleezza Rice to discuss policies on Africa and faith-based community initiatives. When Denny retired from the pastorate in 2005 at the age of 65 he and his beautiful wife Lela chose to move their membership to Strong Tower Bible Church of all places. What an amazing honor for me.

THE STUDENT BECOMES THE TEACHER

Needless to say I was humbled and somewhat intimidated to serve Denny as his pastor. He would say "Preach Preacher" as I spoke on Sunday mornings, and he would often give me "old school" advice after church that I didn't even ask for or solicit. He was now using that toughness in a gentle way. He carried a small pocketknife and he would pull it out and playfully say he would cut anybody who messed with me. I would pinch myself many mornings when I saw him sitting in our congregation because I would sometimes remember where we once stood in our relationship. The truth is, we didn't have a relationship. We were once enemies but now we were friends. Even though I was his pastor, I knew he was my elder.

For the next two and half years, Denny became a court advocate for young people caught up in the legal system. He traveled to Iraq with Scott to visit Christians living there and he ran for Alderman at Large for our city. His campaign leader was a white businessman and his supporters were a wonderful cross section of people. Denny narrowly lost the race and soon found himself in another battle. He suddenly entered into a fight with stage four Pancreatic Cancer at the end of 2007. He told us that this was his storm and Jesus was his Master and Strong God. He loved declaring that he was "tough as a box of rocks" and we believed it. The men of the Empty Hands Fellowship all prayed for Denny's healing at our city's annual Martin Luther King, Jr. Day program in 2008, and in an impromptu moment he spoke mightily from the platform with absolutely no hint of fear. It was a God moment. We all wept knowing it might be his last time addressing all of us. I was taken to preaching school that day because I witnessed a "living, dead man" mouthing the oracles of God. Denny simply wanted God to be glorified in his body whether through life or death.

Denny eventually died on June 16, 2008. Lela called me and I went to the house and viewed his body still sitting in his chair surrounded by his family and friends. There were tears of joy being shed and stories being told that made everyone laugh. It was a very surreal and peaceful moment. David Mullen, who I mentioned earlier in this chapter, was there grieving as well. He considered Denny to be his spiritual father. David and I were joined around Denny's feet by his wife Nicole, their bi-racial daughter Jasmine, and their adopted, black son Max. What a picture of redemption. This was Denny's legacy.

I was blessed, along with Scott, to officiate Denny's home going celebration at Strong Tower Bible Church. The Empty Hands Fellowship guys were all there, too. Those who participated in the service exemplified what Denny came to be known for and that is sweet, beautiful diversity. Rich, poor, Baptists, Presbyterians, blacks, whites, Hispanics, and Native Americans were packed into the church to say their last good byes. We watched film snippets of Denny bargaining a deal for clothes in Africa that made us all laugh. We heard moving testimonies from his family and selections from his comrades Michael Card and Steve Green. As the army bugler serenaded Denny at the Veteran's Cemetery, I committed his body to the earth knowing full well that his spirit was with Jesus.

Only God could turn a situation around like this. Although Denny and I were Christians, we were divided. Although we were both black, we were divided, and as a result, the kingdom of God was divided in our city. Unity only occurred when we humbled ourselves, prayed, and sought God's glory over our personal agendas. As we agree on the major tenants of the faith we can come together because it's always better that way. If we only stay with people who are like us we will foolishly believe that God is only for us. Reach out to another pastor or believer from another church in your community. Share a meal, pray together, and see how and where you can possibly serve God together. That's the only way we'll begin to bridge the divide, one plank at a time.

GOD'S DIVERSE KINGDOM COME THROUGH **GENDER**

"There is neither male nor female…" Galatians 3:28c

1. THE WOMEN IN JESUS' LIFE

Do you remember the biblical account in Luke 7:36-50 when Jesus was invited to the home of a Pharisee named Simon in order to have a meal? An unlikely "sinful" female guest walked in and without asking permission began to anoint and kiss the feet of Jesus in public display. When Simon saw this he said to himself, *"This man, if He were a prophet, would know what manner of woman this is who is touching Him, for she is a sinner"* (Luke 7:39). The religious leaders in Jesus' day sure had a way with words. They conducted themselves as being overly righteous, and "holier than though". The common people could not ascend up to their self imposed glory and rigorous recipe of righteousness. Instead of helping people find God, their belief system and the way they carried themselves caused people to feel that they could never have a relationship with God.

The Bible says when Jesus came on the scene He was totally different than the rabbis, teachers, scribes, and Pharisees of the day. For one thing, Jesus was a friend of sinners (Matthew 11:19). He met people where they were in life. He allowed the people to touch Him in return, including women (Matthew 9:20-22) and children (Matthew 19:13-15). Jesus could also be found in sinners' houses, eating and drinking with them at the table (Matthew 9:10-13). The ordinary people, that is, the sinners, loved Jesus because He didn't condemn them (John 3:17). He didn't condone their behavior either (John 8:11). Somehow through His love and His truthful teachings He was able to compel sinners (II Corinthians 5:14) to walk in the freedom He alone possessed (John 8:32-36) and offered (Galatians 5:1).

Jesus also made it a point to reach out to hurting women during His brief but potent three-year ministerial career. There was Mary and Martha (Luke 10:38-42), Mary Magdalene (Luke 8:2), the widow of Nain (Luke 7:11), the Samaritan woman (John 4:7), the woman "caught" in adultery (John 8:3), the woman with the issue of blood (Matthew 9:20-22), the woman physically oppressed by Satan for 18 years (Luke 13:16), the 12 year-old girl that He raised from the dead (Luke 8:40-42, 49-56), Peter's mother-in-law (Matthew 8:14-15), and of course His mother Mary (John 19:25-27) to name a few. Jesus publicly called women "daughters" as a sign of His acceptance and affirmation of them (Luke 8:48, 13:16).

Whether the women were prostitutes, sinful, sick, or demon-possessed, Jesus made time for them and even laid His hands on them in public (Luke 13:13). This act was unheard of for religious leaders in the first century. Women were viewed as second-class citizens and they were treated with very little respect. The Jews saw women as property on the same level as houses and cattle due to a faulty interpretation of Exodus 20:17. There was usually a double standard in place when it came time to administering justice between men and women, and women usually got cheated (Genesis 38:24-26). A woman could be taken in the very act of adultery and marched towards capital punishment while the guilty male adulterer was somehow visibly invisible (John 8:3-4). Women were considered as mere objects of scorn, especially if they could not produce male children (Genesis 16:2, 30:3). Even the disciples were surprised to see Jesus talking openly with the woman of Samaria (John 4:27).

I believe women supported Jesus so strongly (Luke 8:1-3) because He genuinely appreciated them. For once, they met a religious leader who treated them with dignity, honor, and respect as He showed them the way of God. Not once was Jesus ever accused of inappropriate conduct or contact with a woman. Jesus valued and esteemed the women He came in contact with regardless of their background or race (Matthew 15:21-28). Women loved Jesus. He was a fresh drink in a parched place. The love women had for Jesus stationed them at His cross when the men fled (Matthew 26:31, 56, 75, 27:55-56). It was the women's dedication that had them come to the tomb early Sunday morning (Matthew 28:1) when the male disciples were shut up indoors, fearfully hiding from the Jews (John 20:19).

WOMEN SHOULD ALWAYS PRAY

Luke 18:1 says, *"Then he spoke a parable to them, that men always ought to pray and not lose heart."* The King James Version says of the same verse, *"Men should always pray and not faint."* When challenging and inspiring His male disciples to pray, Jesus chose to use an illustration about a persistent woman to get His point across. Once again, Jesus proved that He was not your typical kind of rabbi. He was willing to go against culture when culture went against the kingdom. Jesus used a woman to teach men how to pray just like He used children to teach adults about the kingdom (Matthew 18:1-5) and the faith of foreigners to inspire faith in His own people Israel (Matthew 8:5-10). Jesus had a tendency of putting the most unlikely people on pedestals for the sake of challenging the status quo and stressing the message of the kingdom. Jesus was well rounded, far from square, and no manmade theological or cultural box could ever define Him or confine Him. Jesus knew the power of a woman's prayers because His mother and other women would pray and cry out for Him in His darkest hour (Luke 23:27-31).

There's an old Negro spiritual that starts off saying, "My mother prayed for me, had me on her mind, took the time to pray for me. I'm so glad she prayed. I'm so glad she prayed. Took the time and prayed for me." The spiritual then goes through the rest of the family by saying my father prayed for me, my brother and my sister prayed for me, and then it says the preacher prayed for me. I think it is significant that the song starts off with the prayers of the mother and not the prayers of the father. In many African American homes then and unfortunately now, mothers and especially grandmothers carry the spiritual weight. It was always common to hear kids say, "I'm going to church with my grandmother." Acclaimed singer Helen Baylor recalls in her song, "Helen's Testimony", that she had a praying grandmother. She attributes her grandmother's prayers for getting her out of a life of sin and off drugs.

LEAVE HER ALONE

Our women often see what men don't see, and they often do what men would never do. Jesus affirmed this on the eve of His arrest and crucifixion. An unnamed woman came to Simon the leper's house and anointed Jesus with costly oil as He sat at the table (Mark 14:3). This lady gave Jesus her best offering and He gladly received it. The religiously rigid men around Jesus missed the meaning of that mighty moment. The men were indignant and ascribed a dollar amount to the woman's foolish display and called her actions a waste of money and probably even time (Mark 14:4). They even tried to disguise their disgust for this woman's waste by pretending to possess a concern for ministry to the poor (Mark 14:5). In the wake of Jesus' dreadful hour He had to sit and listen to His men sharply criticize and scold this woman sharply.

The men didn't see Jesus the way this lady saw Him. In her eyes, Jesus was worth the sacrifice because of the sacrifice He was about to make on the cross. In her eyes, Jesus was about to be broken and poured out for her sins so the least she could do was to break a bottle of something precious and costly and pour it out on Him as symbol of her love, devotion, and appreciation for Him. In a matter of hours the Father would accept the blood sacrifice of His Son as a pleasing aroma and acceptable offering for sin (I John 2:2). This unnamed lady saw that about Jesus but the men didn't. Today's men need to see through our ladies' eyes sometimes, especially when it comes to worshipping Jesus. Our male pride and egos cause us to miss the Christ quite often, especially in corporate worship.

Jesus plainly defended the woman and said, *"Let her alone. Why do you trouble her? She has done a good work for Me. For you have the poor always, and whenever you wish you may do them good; but Me you do not have always. She has done what she could. She has come beforehand to anoint my body for burial Assuredly, I say to you, wherever this gospel is preached in the whole world, what this woman has done will also be told as a memorial to her"* (Mark 14:6-9).

I have heard the gospel preached all over the world and I have been fortunate to preach all over the world myself, but not once have I heard a male preacher of the gospel honor this woman in a sermon. Not once have I ever called attention to this certain lady's actions, and I feel like most men still miss the point that Jesus was trying so hard to make. Had this been a man anointing Jesus this way, I'm sure we would hear it and see statues all over the place depicting this moment in time.

Nevertheless, Jesus leaves all of us men with the admonition to uplift, speak about, and call attention to the involvement of women in God's Diverse Kingdom. He expects for us to treat, honor, and include women the way He so wonderfully did. Most men love a good challenge. Let's start making legitimate, healthy strides in this department.

2. DIGNITY WITHOUT COMPROMISE

Every church, and every believer for that matter, must have a thoughtful, biblically sound perspective on the matter of women's role in leadership and pulpit ministry in today's church. Women ministers are appearing more and more frequently today and are making a major difference. Some say their impactful presence in pulpit leadership is for better while others say for worse, but what does the Bible say? Is there a balance that can be achieved?

Our church has been blessed with one of the best women's ministry leaders in the entire world! Kristi McLelland has been with me for over 12 years as my longest tenured staff person. She is a seminary graduate, author, motivator, and a tremendously gifted speaker. Hailing as a white woman from Mississippi, her presence in the life of the church makes our vision for the Diverse Kingdom all the more real and effective. I am not ashamed to admit that Kristi is the best teacher in our church. Kristi has shown nothing but love and respect for me ever since I've known her. She has never demanded the pulpit or desired a pastoral position. On occasion, I ask her and other women in our body with similar dispositions to minister God's Word to our congregation on Sunday mornings. I believe Kristi's spirit, theological understanding, presence on staff, and strong involvement in our church has allowed our ministry to bypass many gender wars that are prevalent in many parishes today where women feel slighted. I didn't always have this position of female inclusion in the pulpit, but over time God was able to balance me out. Kristi's loving demeanor and not a theological argument opened up my eyes to see the Diverse Kingdom. I hope you can begin to see what I now see and enjoy.

THE LIBERAL LEFT VERSUS THE RIGID RIGHT

As in most cases there are usually two extremes. Even though the Bible encourages us from taking extremes (Ecclesiastes 7:18 NIV), there are still the proverbial far right and far left perspectives that are all too common. The far right tends to be ultra-conservative and women in these settings cannot speak publicly at all in the church because of incorrect interpretations of Scripture that stem from male chauvinism. Some churches contend that women cannot walk on the platform of the church or stand behind the pulpit for any reason for fear of being in the place of male authority. Usually these women are told that they *"shall not wear anything that pertains to a man…"* In our culture this means that a woman cannot wear pants under any circumstances. Is *that* what Moses meant when he wrote Deuteronomy 22:5 and gave the Old Covenant to the Israelites? Did Moses even know what pants were? Were pants even invented at this time? In Moses' day all of the men wore clothing that would be perceived as "dresses" today. We must be careful about not reading our contemporary idioms and personal biases into the Bible.

What about makeup? For so long women were told that since Jezebel painted her eyes and used her beauty as a tool of sexual seduction (II Kings 9:30), Christian women should refrain from the use of makeup. Therefore cosmetics ("cosmos" in the Greek) are considered by some in the body of Christ to be worldly, and these extremists often call make up "the devil's paint". Many conservative Christians consider women getting a perm in their hair as being unnatural and worldly. Sadly, women in these churches are trapped in a time warp, never catching up to the culture with the hopes of one day changing culture for Christ by having a hand in setting the fashion trends.

Conservative churches that do allow women to wear pants and make up may even allow them to teach women and children in Sunday School, sing solos in the choir, and give the church's announcements at a podium away from the pulpit. These are usually seen as "women's jobs". More progressive churches may even allow a woman to lead worship but she must limit her comments before and after songs or else she may be accused of "usurping" male authority or teaching men in the congregation. But when you scale it down, the woman *is* teaching men and women through song as she leads the congregation. If she explains a song, reads Scripture, or gives a brief personal testimony, she's technically teaching. The real question behind all of this is: Can a Christian man learn anything about God from a woman? If the answer is "yes", as it should be, why can't that man learn something from a woman at church? Is church limited to an in-house, formal gathering on Sunday or are we to be the church everyday everywhere?

The opposite extreme, which is usually borne out of a reaction to oppression, adapted a loose, subjective interpretation of Scripture on this matter of a woman's role in public ministry. Galatians 3:28 which says, *"There is neither Jew nor Greek, there is neither slave nor free, there is neither male nor female; for you are all one in Christ Jesus"*, somehow became the primary verse to support sameness of role and function in the local church between men and women. In other words, if a man can be a pastor, a woman can be a pastor, also. This verse was interpreted to erase all ethnic distinctions between Jews and Greeks. Many non-Jewish Christians overlook the biblical and historical presence of Israel by erroneously claiming promises made to Israel for themselves. When God saves people from their sins they don't stop being Jewish or Gentile. When slaves came to Christ in first century Rome or sixteenth century America, their societal statuses weren't changed overnight if at all. I believe the point Paul is making in Galatians 3:28 is that racial, social, and gender variances are not meant to bring division among followers of Christ. Our differences shouldn't really matter. In Christ we are all one, but being one doesn't mean we are expected to be the same. Being one in Christ doesn't mean we're supposed to do the same things or have the same things.

In our post-modern era there is a self-imposed pressure for the church to stay relevant and in step with the world. That's not always a bad motivation, however, we cannot allow the world's standards to cause us to compromise Biblical truth in the process of being relevant. Post-modernism is showing up in the Christian's approach to science, theology, relationships, parenting, entertainment, the arts, literature, politics, and church government. Like never before, there is a newfound push to include women in the office of elder or pastor in the local church. In the name of modernity, churches are becoming more and more open to female inclusion in official leadership.

I have discovered that men and women who hold to a more liberal view of women's involvement in pastoral leadership are quick to leave the Scriptures in developing their position. They tend to formulate their perspective primarily against the backdrop of contemporary reasoning. They go about seeking verses of Scripture to support their view. And when they do quote the Scriptures, especially the writings of Paul, I feel they interpret the passages as only being relevant to Paul's initial listeners and not to our audience. For instance, they will discuss the unique cultural phenomenon of the day when Paul wrote to Ephesus or Corinth, but they will say those Scriptures are unique to those churches and not our era and should be interpreted as such. Their reason is, "If women are out of order for speaking in today's church, I suppose women are out of order if they don't wear head coverings, too. If you are going to quote Paul on one point, you have to quote him on all points." When our hermeneutics revolve around this kind of infantile rationale, it is no wonder the church is wide open to being blown around by the latest trends.

THE FAMILY AS GOD INTENDED

The traditional or nuclear family took a tremendous blow in the eighties and nineties. Nowadays a family consists of whatever one wants it to be. Nevertheless, God's intention is that the family consists of one husband and one wife for life (Genesis 2:24), but in today's world of relativism there can be two mommies or two daddies at home. In most cases, homes are likely to be led by one parent and that's usually a mother or a grandmother. These numbers are even more staggering among ethnic minorities. I recently heard a story where one man visited another man in prison. The man behind bars asked the visiting gentleman to bring him a card for Mother's Day on his next visit so that he could sign it and send it to his mother. The visitor was kind enough to oblige the prisoner. When the other inmates found out about this act of kindness they asked the man to do the same thing for them. The man brought in fifty cards to give away to the prisoners and send out to their mothers for Mother's Day. How beautiful! But when Father's day came along, not one inmate made a request to send a card to his father. I would also be interested in knowing how many of those men behind bars received cards or visits from their children on Father's Day.

When the church is brought into the discussion, many of them, especially churches comprised of ethnic minorities, tend to be greatly populated with women and some of the men who do attend church are often effeminate. Several men are quick to lose interest in church because they don't feel the pastor or the programs can relate to them. An obvious void of male participation and leadership occurs, so women pick up leading in church the way they were forced to lead at home. Women will not only nurture, but they will lead the family if the man is not there to do so. She may still lead if the man is present in the home but is passive. Women will step up when men step back or step out. Women, like Hagar in the Bible, are survivors by nature and they will get from God what they need and then give to their children with or without the aid of a man (see Genesis 16 and 21). The example of Deborah from Judges became an inspiration for women (Judges 4-5). She was forced to lead when men were there like Barak, who should have led but would not lead (Judges 4:8). However, Deborah had a proper understanding of the way healthy military leadership and the national achievement of a goal should work in the Jewish culture (Judges 4:9). Deborah understood the importance of male leadership and she tried to push Barak forward, yet at the same time she would not allow God's program to stop because of the absence of solid, male leadership.

The high rise of women in church leadership today is due in part to the absence of proper male leadership in the home. Women who are forced into leadership at home due to the male void have carried that mentality into the church and have become pastors and elders of churches. When gifted women are not used or acknowledged by their churches and denominations they usually find places that will acknowledge and use them. Sometimes they end up starting their own churches, movements, and denominations themselves. Churches that don't accept the view of women being able to serve as pastors, elders, or bishops are looked upon as being out of touch, behind, and old fashioned. The challenge for the church today is no different than what Jesus faced. How does a church involve the precious and powerful gifts God placed in women without compromising the basic Biblical tenants of the family or church government to do so?

WE ARE ONE BUT NOT THE SAME—WE ARE EQUAL BUT DIFFERENT

We must begin with the premise that men and women are intrinsically equal before God in all matters pertaining to humanity (Genesis 1:26-27) and redemption (Galatians 3:28). A woman is not more than a man or less than a man when it comes to personhood. Male and female are equal in essence; however, equality of essence doesn't mean sameness of role or function. That is the key to shaping a balanced understanding. Men and women can be one without being the same or doing the same thing in the church. We are equal but different, and that's okay.

Within God's institution of marriage He has prescribed various roles for the two participants. *"In the beginning"*, Jesus said, *"God made them male and female"* (Matthew 19:4). One man and one woman is the only acceptable combination for God's institution of marriage. Anything else would be unnatural (Romans 1:24-32), an abomination (Leviticus 18:22), and punishable by God (Hebrews 13:4). A husband and wife are equal in every way but God ordained that they play different roles in the marriage covenant. The husband's primary role is to be the *"head"* (Ephesians 5:23). Headship never means lording over another person. Headship doesn't mean that a man is better than a woman. Headship doesn't mean male dominance or intimidation. Rather, headship in the kingdom of God always speaks of responsibility, humility, love, and service. Jesus demonstrated His Headship when He served and washed the feet of the disciples (John 13:1-7).

The woman's primary role in marriage is to be that of *"helper"* (Genesis 2:18, 20). Helper doesn't mean that a woman is "less than" her counterpart. This same Hebrew word is used to describe God as being Israel's helper (Psalm 121:1-2). God knew that men would need lots of help; therefore women (Genesis 2:18) and the Holy Spirit (John 14:16) were His answers! God knew women needed shepherding and protection so husbands (Ephesians 5:23) and the Lord (Psalm 23:1) are His provisions for them!

Since there is a clear designation of roles and responsibilities laid forth in the Bible by God, the architect, and manufacturer of marriage, it would behoove all married people to adhere to His mandates. In order to get the optimum amount of blessings to flow unhindered through the marriage covenant we must do things God's way. To disregard or reverse God's general plan for the family brings confusion and a lack of blessing. When the wife operates as the leader and primary decision maker of the home it causes unnecessary chaos. When the husband becomes a passive responder, the home is out of order. The home may function, but it won't function as God intended. Women who tend to be stronger leaders than their husbands must learn to personally and willfully yield rightful authority to their husbands. Men who tend to be passive and non-assertive must learn to tactfully love and lead their wives as Christ loves and leads the church. God has ordained that husbands need to step up and wives need to step back.

The home is the microcosm for the church. The family is the number one unit for society and the church for that matter. As our homes go, so goes the church. As the church goes, so goes the community. In fact, stipulations are placed upon a man's home life to determine whether or not he can lead in God's house (I Timothy 3:4-5). So if a man is called by God to lead his wife and his home, why would God turn around and have a woman lead the church house and church family?

WHAT ABOUT JESUS?

As we said in the last chapter, Jesus valued women and included them in God's program like no other rabbi in his day. But keep in mind, Jesus didn't compromise God's standard in order to "validate" women through hierarchical promotions. He did not appoint one woman to be a part of His leadership team of the Twelve Apostles (Luke 6:12-16). That truth needs to be greatly considered. It can't be said that Jesus didn't want to offend the Pharisees in that male dominant culture by having women on His team because Jesus never allowed the religious establishment to hinder His agenda on any other issue. In fact, if Jesus' first coming was in this "all inclusive" era His leadership team would have still been comprised of all males. Why? It would have been unnatural to have women in primary places of spiritual leadership because He would have contradicted the order of the home that He established in Genesis 2 and Psalm 128. Also, with the church being built on the foundation of the apostles (Ephesians 2:20), He would have opened the door to confusion and controversy for future generations. Jesus would not and could not contradict His creative order for the sake of total female accommodation or to be politically correct.

For Jesus, He could love, value, esteem, and depend upon women in the ministry. At the same time He would not compromise His creative order of male leadership in the domestic home and in the church house to do so. Jesus had a beautiful balance in how He instilled dignity in women without compromising God's standard in the process. That's our challenge for today. God is a God of order but Satan is the author of disorder and confusion (I Corinthians 14:33). Therefore, any kind of female posturing over a man in the home or in the church is essentially satanically influenced (I Timothy 2:14, 5:14-15). Satan, who is a fallen, un-submissive angelic being, despised, rejected, and resisted established authority as ordained by God. He purposefully tempted and influenced Eve with the folly that he himself fell from heaven with. He deceived Eve to step out from under God and from under her husband. Satan influenced Eve to become the head and primary decision maker of the family (Genesis 3:1-7). This brought chaos. Another sad thing is that Adam was there and he allowed the devil to turn his home upside down because he was passive. It's a shame when men are present in the home but passive. Adam should have done what God did in heaven and that was to expel the serpent from Eden. Adam went wrong when he listened to his wife over the command he received from the Lord. Subsequently, their home was never the same (Genesis 3:17).

If you notice, nothing happened when Eve bit the forbidden fruit, but everything changed for the worse when Adam bit the fruit because he was the God-established, federal leader of the family. Their eyes were now opened and they saw their nakedness! When God came upon the scene of the crash His first question was, *"Adam, where are you (Genesis 3:9)?"* God didn't ask for Adam and Eve because God always operates by the order of the family that He established. Unlike Satan, God went to the head for answers first. Eve would eventually be held accountable to God for her own actions but she would not be held responsible for the family breakdown. That was Adam's responsibility as the leader (Romans 5:12).

One of the effects of the fall would be that women would always struggle with wanting to step out in front and lead their husbands. No matter how much the wife desires to rule over her husband, God says that the husband shall rule over her (Genesis 3:16). Period. The wife may be far more gifted than her husband in many respects but she doesn't have the authorization by God to usurp or replace her husband as the leader. Once again, the wife must constantly and intentionally step back and the husband must constantly and intentionally step up. I believe this fleshly urge for a woman to rule in the home also manifests in a woman's urge to lead inappropriately in the church house. Please stay with me.

With great grace and wisdom Jesus brought respect, honor, and dignity to women during His earthly ministry that even surprised His disciples (John 4:27). He championed and redeemed the status of women in society. Jesus did this through His public dealings and affirmations of them in a male dominant and sometimes abusive culture (John 4:4-26, 8:1-11). He often used women in positive ways as examples in His teachings (Luke 15:8-10, 18:1-8), and it was women who helped finance the disciples' ministry (Luke 8:1-3). But most significantly it was women whom Jesus appeared to first when He resurrected (Luke 24:1-11).

He went on to tell the women in His resurrected state to, *"Go and tell my brothers to go to Galilee, and there they will see Me."* (Matt. 28:10). Jesus told women to communicate a message about God to men. The women were even told to give the men instructions and teach them about the future plans of Jesus concerning where to meet. Do you think that was purposeful? Yes it was! Jesus knew the nature of men (John 2:24-25) and He knew the disciples would not initially heed the women's message (Mark 16:11, Luke 24:9-11) due to their cultural upbringing (see also Acts 12:11-15). In this case, if the men had not listened to the women proclaim the truth about the resurrection of Jesus they would have sat in a state of ignorance and lacked a blessed experience with God.

This shows us that men will sometimes not listen to God if His instructions are coming through a woman. Jewish men transferred their negative views of women over to God. It is true that women in that culture were unlearned as far as receiving a formal education. They were considered primarily as offspring bearing creatures like oxen and other livestock. Jewish men compared women with animals because of a poor interpretation of the 10th commandment which said, *"You shall not covet your neighbor's house; you shall not covet your neighbor's wife, nor his male servant, nor his female servant, nor his ox, nor his donkey, nor anything that is your neighbor's."*

Jesus had His male disciples pray together with the women in the upper room (Acts 1:12-14) in anticipation of a new day that the Spirit would bring about through the church. That kind of gender inclusivity in the sphere of spiritual activity was unheard of in the temple and in the synagogues. That's why the church is the new wineskin for the new wine! God's Spirit was poured out on all flesh, both men and women, and the women would be given the ability from God to prophesy (Acts 2:17-18). There is obviously a place for women to prophesy to the body at large.

WHAT ABOUT PAUL?

The Apostle Paul had the same approach to women in the ministry that Jesus had. He valued, implored, and recognized women's contributions (Romans 16:1-6, 12-16). Paul knew that a woman didn't have to be a pastor or elder in order to be viewed as a man's equal. According to the Apostle, she is man's equal and man is her equal (I Corinthians 11:11-12), but God has designated that they have different roles in the home and in the church.

We must understand that when a woman desires to be a pastor or elder of a church, that desire, as strong and sincere as it may be, did not come from God but from her flesh (I Timothy 3:1-7). Paul made it very clear that *"if a man desires the position of a bishop* (i.e. pastor/elder; Acts 20:17, 28), *he desires a good work"*. The word for *"man"* is *"tis"* which like *"anthropos"* can speak of a male specifically or of humankind in general based on the context. Paul further made his point of male leadership in the position of elder by saying that this man must be *"the husband* ("andras") *of one wife"* (I Timothy 3:2). No woman qualifies to be a husband or to have a wife.

Two different Greek words are used for *"desire"* in I Timothy 3:1. The first word means to reach out, aspire to, or to go after, like in an external action. The second Greek word for *"desire"* is "epithumia" which means a strong inward desire or craving. This word is also translated as "lust" in other Scripture depending upon the context. When the two words are put together it means that a man qualifies to be a pastor, elder, or bishop when he outwardly pursues the office because he is driven by a strong internal desire or calling from God. God works in the man and the man works the calling out (Philippians 2:12-13). Having desire alone does not make a man qualified to be an elder, pastor, or bishop. There are plenty of elders and pastors in places of authority who are not called or qualified. And like these men, women can have a strong desire to be a pastor or elder and still not be eligible. The desire doesn't necessitate or legitimize the call. As mentioned, the desire to be a pastor is from her flesh and not from God because He would never give a woman a calling or desire that contradicts His written Word.

This order for the local church that the apostle Paul wrote to Timothy about was to be the standard for all churches according to I Timothy 3:14-15, *"These things I write to you, though I hope to come to you shortly; but if I am delayed, I write so that you may know how you ought to conduct yourself in the house of God, which is the church of the living God, the pillar and foundation of the truth."*

THE "PROBLEMED" PASSAGE

But wasn't it Paul who said, *"And I do not permit a woman to teach or to have authority over a man, but to be in silence"* (I Timothy 2:12)? It has mainly been this passage that has caused the tension between believers in Christ when the topics of women, church leadership, and pulpit ministry are discussed. The left would say that Paul himself was a chauvinist among other things. The leftists would go on to say that these menial mandates have no bearings on us today because we live in a different era. The right wing would say that Paul was correct about his assessment and women shouldn't teach a man God's Word under any circumstances. At a casual glance, I Timothy 2:12 could say a lot of things, but first, let's determine what Paul is NOT saying in this passage:

1) Paul is <u>NOT</u> saying that a woman cannot teach ever or else he would contradict what he said in Titus 2:4 *"…the older women likewise, that they be reverent in behavior, not slanderers, not given to much wine, teachers of good things- that they may admonish* (i.e. teach) *the young women to love their husbands, to love their children…"* Again, a rigid reading of this verse could imply that Paul did not permit women to teach at all and we know that's not true.

2) Paul is <u>NOT</u> saying that a woman cannot ever teach a man data about God because as mentioned, women taught men after the resurrection of Jesus in John 20:17-18. In Acts 18:26, Aquila and his wife Priscilla taught the man Apollos the basics of the faith. According to Romans 16:3-5, Aquila and Priscilla also had a church that met in their home. The passage doesn't say they were the "pastors" of that house church however, but it does speak of their availability to God. In today's paradigm, they would qualify to be small group leaders in a cell model.

3) Paul is <u>NOT</u> saying that a woman cannot teach a man in church or else he would contradict what he said in I Corinthians 11:5 *"But every woman who prays or prophesies with her head uncovered dishonors her head..."* There are times we learn theology through prayers and since women were now able to be included in the learning of theology with the inception of the church, they could pray publicly. To prophesy means to tell forth a message from God to the people of God, or to foretell a future message about God to the people of God. Prophecy, like preaching, contains teachings about Jesus (Revelation 19:10). Therefore, a woman can teach the congregation about God and His ways through a testimony, a song, a prayer, a play, and yes, a sermon.

Secondly, let's determine what Paul IS saying:

1) Paul <u>IS</u> saying that a woman cannot teach in the church in any capacity with the purpose of taking authority <u>over</u> a man. This verb "usurp" is a unique word, used only one time in Scripture. Its uses in antiquity suggest a forceful taking over of something that does not rightfully belong to the one doing the taking. This looks at the attitude of the woman teacher and not just the act of teaching per se. This calls attention to the woman's spirit, and not to her ability to teach. Women with obtrusive attitudes are usually defensive and combative when discussing this topic because in their heart of hearts they know they are out of order. Their attitude exposes the natural dysfunction of operating outside of God's perfect plan. These women tend to resist strong, godly male leadership, classifying them as narrow or intimidated. It is highly probable that women who serve as pastors experienced poor, absent, or abusive male leadership in the home and the church while growing up. Therefore to be "under a man" in any capacity is not acceptable.

2) Paul <u>IS</u> saying that a woman cannot teach in the church with the purpose of taking authority <u>from</u> a man. That is, she cannot teach from the authoritative position and office of elder/bishop/pastor (interchangeable terms of the one man- Acts 20:17, 28). The office of pastor/elder/bishop is reserved only for men (I Timothy 3:1-2, Titus 1:6), but men or pastors are not the only people who can teach in the church. As previously stated, women can teach in the church, but they can't hold or teach from the position of bishop, elder, or pastor. Therefore, it would be incorrect to ordain a woman to be a

pastor, bishop, or elder in a local church under any circumstance. If able, spiritual men are not present, then a woman may step in to lead and teach the church until God supplies a male shepherd to direct the affairs of the church (I Timothy 5:17). She would not need to be called "pastor" during that interim time even if she functions as one.

But the question is: Once the right man does come to the church will the woman who once led temporarily be able to pull back from leading the church and give the authority to the man without causing a church split? She will be able to do so if her attitude was right from the beginning and if she didn't inordinately strive to attain the office of pastor that is designated for men only. A woman who understands this understands kingdom order.

The same is true in a single parent home led by a woman. A woman will lead because she has no choice, but if she ever gets married, she will have to submit the "reigns" of the family to her husband. This will mean that the husband will lead the home and together he and his wife will oversee the discipline of her children even if they aren't his biologically. Many blended families struggle to survive or never begin because of this challenge. A woman must truly trust a man and God if she is going to willingly hand over the authority of the home. For the marriage covenant to be what God intended she must or else failure is imminent.

IS THIS TEACHING RELEVANT FOR TODAY?

Some have argued and said, "That was first century Ephesus and this is 21st century America. Those directives are not necessary today." That kind of rationalizing is dangerous because it violates the basic rules of Bible interpretation. But regardless, Paul, seeming to anticipate that question referred to creative order in I Timothy 2:13 which says, *"For Adam was formed first, then Eve."* Paul wrote in I Corinthians 11:3, *"But I want you to know that the head of every man is Christ, the head of woman is man, and the head of Christ is God."* The order of creation is a biblical and kingdom principle that transcends culture and time.

We know that Jesus is equal to the Father (John 10:30, Philippians 2:6), but He voluntarily placed Himself under the Father in submission (John 6:38). So too the wife is equal to her husband (Galatians 3:28), but she must voluntarily place herself under her husband in submission (Ephesians 5:22). In our attempt to uplift women from past sins of abuse, discrimination, and chauvinism we cannot compromise God's standard in the home or the church to do so. Equality of essence doesn't mean sameness of role or function. There is a beauty in the balance if we are willing to find it.

Even though I believe I have sound, biblical interpretations in this area, I still gladly fellowship and work alongside women that are ordained elders, pastors, and bishops. They usually don't ask for my opinion or approval for the work they feel God has called them to accomplish. These women are my sisters in Christ and I love them. Our diversity as men and women is what makes us unique. The Diverse Kingdom has many exemplary, electrifying women of God doing the Lord's work. This matter is not a hill worth dying on for me. There are many battles to fight and I don't mind if the person in the foxhole with me is a woman pastor. I only care if she is shooting in the same direction, at the same enemy, and with the same ammunition. She can also trust that I will not shift my focus and shoot her in the back.

I am fortunate to lead a church that has amazing women who understand and support God's paradigm for leadership in the home and the church. Without them, our church would not function at its full potential. As Paul the Apostle relied upon Phoebe (Romans 16:1-2), so I rely upon our female deacons to handle important matters in our church. Women like Loretta McDonald, Tammy Lenox, Tammy Conover, and Beth Blinn are often found laboring in trenches with or without men. The sooner men and women see that they are not in competition with one another the greater our experience of oneness will be. Our church proves that women are happy serving as long as they are respected.

Strong Tower Bible Church has women like Debbie French, Carolyn Riviere, Laura Cooksey, and Alisa Malone frequently leading us on missions' trips to Ghana, West Africa. Only Philip's four prophesying daughters are their rivals (Acts 21:9). You may come one Sunday and hear Darlene Dyson passionately preaching God's word and calling our attention to widows and orphans in Sudan. My wife Dorena, along with Erica Mitchell, Sherri Gragg, and Stephanie Fitzgerald teach classes and conduct seminars for our church on various topics that would make prophetesses Huldah (II Kings 22:14) and Anna (Luke 2:36) look on with anticipation. I can go on and on about the caliber of women God has graced our church with. There are many women who effectively use their gifts by operating according to God's design for the family and the church. Not one of these ladies is an elder, bishop, or pastor. They don't desire these roles. And as I stand up with my sisters in the Lord, I am pleased to say God's Diverse Kingdom is coming through our church without compromise.

3. MALE AND FEMALE AND NOTHING ELSE

I don't believe it is possible to have a book on diversity in the 21st century and not cover the topic of homosexuality. The word diversity has taken on a different meaning than what it used to mean fifteen or twenty years ago. Diversity has now come to embody the acceptance, tolerance, and inclusion of homosexuals and their lifestyle in all spheres and walks of life. Diversity training in major corporations and institutions of higher learning has become commonplace. It teaches people to not only understand, but to also accept differences in religions, races, cultures, and sexual orientations as normal expressions of people living in a free society.

We know by now that homosexuals see themselves as a minority people group in America in need of social benefits, legal protection, and civil rights just like African Americans, Asians, Latino, and handicap people groups. More and more people are coming out of the proverbial closet and they are airing their laundry in a climate of political correctness, social acceptance, and moral relativism. Politicians have taken into account the "gay vote" when campaigning. Teachers have to be sensitive to the possibility that some of their students come from same-sex homes. On the other hand, parents send their kids to school being mindful of the fact that their child's teacher or the school's curriculum may now embrace and support homosexuality as an acceptable lifestyle. Professional counselors routinely tell patients struggling with homosexual feelings that they were born that way, that they cannot change, and that they should simply learn to affirm their feelings.

I know for a fact that there are many good people struggling with homosexual urges, tendencies, feelings, thoughts and actions. These people are our family members, friends, colleagues, co-workers, church leaders, and church members. They have questions and concerns and they don't know where they can turn. Unfortunately, the church has been the last place people struggling with homosexual tendencies can go to find real help. Instead of compassion they have typically found condemnation, rejection, and ridicule. This only serves to widen the chasm and increase the possibility of rebellion. Men and women struggling with same sex issues get treated as if their plight is contagious, and contrary to popular belief, homosexual sin is not the unpardonable sin.

I APOLOGIZE

That being said, I want to take this time to apologize to anyone who has been emotionally hurt or verbally bashed by a fearful, ignorant, insensitive, and insecure preacher or Christian. I apologize from the bottom of my heart on their behalf. I am also sorry for anyone reading this chapter that was molested, raped, or sexually abused at a young age. Psychologists have said that exposure to sex in an incorrect fashion or even early in life can produce a distressed sexual orientation. I am so sorry for what may have happened to you against your will by someone that you trusted.

And as you accept my apology, I pray that you accept my personal conviction on the subject. I believe good people can be confused. I believe sincere people can be sincerely wrong, and I believe homosexual behavior is a sin before God. God will never condone homosexual sins. He loves people too much to not tell them the truth and make a way through His Son to set them free from the path of destruction they are on. I apologize for how people may have mistreated you along the way, but I do not apologize for the truth. Like Jesus felt about the Nicolaitans in Revelation 2:6, I hate the deeds of homosexuals, but I don't hate homosexuals. Like Jesus, I love the homosexual just like I love the adulterer, but I will not tolerate or condone either one's lifestyle preferences. And neither do I tolerate adultery when it arises in my sinful heart. Jesus is my only remedy in those times of sexual temptation.

Some Christians have gone on record as to say that God made them gay and if you have a problem with them you need to take it up with God. Gay men have said, "Ever since I can remember I have had these desires to be with another man." Lesbian women have said, "I have been attracted to women my whole life. I have always been somewhat masculine. Ever since I was a child I have felt like I was a man trapped inside of a woman's body." The subtlety of this message places the blame on God and not upon the individual.

THE SILENCE OF THE LAMB

The apparent silence of Jesus on this matter has caused many to suggest that since Jesus didn't condemn homosexuality He must have been tolerant of it.

In their minds Jesus' silence must mean acceptance. Silence usually means consent but not for Jesus. That is a poor line of reasoning and it is an even worse approach to sound interpretation of the Bible. As far as His recorded words are concerned, Jesus didn't speak specifically on the topics of rape, incest, kidnapping, mass murder, pedophilia, abortion, or cocaine and drug usage to name a few. And what many fail to realize is that the entire Bible is the Word of God and not just what Jesus said. So whether truth comes from the mouth of Jesus or the mouths of Moses, David, or Paul, we must remember that all Scripture is given by the inspiration of God and is profitable for doctrine, reproof, and correction (II Timothy 3:16).

Although Jesus didn't specifically address homosexuality we have to ask ourselves, what did He address by way of sex, relationships, and the family? Once we know what Jesus stands for we will soon discover what He opposes. Jesus is clearly supportive of male and female sexual relationships being expressed within the confines of marriage (Hebrews 13:4). The only sex that God sanctions, ordains, blesses, and approves is sex between a husband and his wife. Period. Therefore, fornication is a sin. Adultery is a sin, and homosexual intercourse is a sin. Sin is anything we do, think, or say that goes against the holy nature of God and His commandments. Sin is missing the mark and falling short of God's standard, glory, and perfection. We need a savior because we all sin and hurt ourselves and other people, not to mention the heart of God.

In Matthew chapter 19, the Pharisees asked Jesus about His perspective on divorce. Jesus took them back to the beginning of God's creation and plan for marriage and said, *"Have you not read that he who made them at the beginning made them male and female, and said, 'for this cause shall a man leave his father and mother and be joined to his wife, and the two shall become one flesh'"?* Jesus made it clear that the blueprint for marriage and the family is one man and one woman, permanently married to each other in the sight of God. Jesus went back to the beginning where it was male and female and nothing else. Any other definition or expression of marriage and the family is totally unacceptable. It doesn't matter how nice, loving, religious, or sincere the people may be. And even though we are lulled and seduced by the media to be tolerant towards every kind of sexual preference and expression, Christians cannot get sucked into this kind of compromise. Disagreeing with this growing and pervasive alternative lifestyle causes followers of the biblical Jesus to be viewed as insensitive, narrow, intolerant, and full of hatred and bigotry. My unwillingness to endorse homosexuality as an acceptable way of life does not make me homophobic or fascist. I can love you as a person without accepting your behavior. Jesus did that (Revelation 2:6, 15). You can't force homosexuality on me or anyone else for that matter anymore than I can force Christianity on you. So go ahead and keep standing for what you believe in because I don't plan on changing either.

DOES GOD MAKE PEOPLE GAY?

If we say that God makes people gay that removes the moral responsibility from the gay person to repent and change. If we say that God makes people gay we are saying that God accepts homosexual behavior. If we say that God makes people gay then that means that homosexual unions should eventually be accepted and legally recognized in every state in America the same way heterosexual marriages are accepted and legally recognized. If we say that God makes people gay then that means they are a minority in need of civil rights, benefits, and protection under law just like ethnic minorities. If we say that God makes people gay then those who oppose this notion have a problem with God and not with the gay person. But as we'll see, being gay is a lifestyle choice and not a birthright.

To find a biological cause like a "gay gene" or a "gay hormone" would give credence to the notion of "I was born this way." A gay gene would say that homosexuality is not a sin but a biological condition, and as such, homosexuals should be entitled to legal and social recognition as any other minority in our country in need of rights, privileges, and protection under law. Studies that have been done thus far to find biological causes for homosexuality have all been inconclusive.

We are all influenced by the society in which we live. Where we choose to live, what we eat, how we dress, how we talk, how we think and even how we relate to one another sexually are all affected by society. Through the media, education, politics, music, and entertainment we are consciously and intentionally fed an agenda that is contrary to God's agenda for our lives. Through subtle images and overt messages we are constantly bombarded with the plight of the homosexual so that we might embrace their lifestyle choice.

SPIRITUAL CAUSES FOR HOMOSEXUALITY

So where does people behaving with homosexual actions come from? It all begins with our fallen, sinful nature. Ultimately, homosexuality is a manifestation of the imbedded sin nature just as alcoholism, immorality, and lying happen to be as well. Sin has so spoiled every aspect of our being spiritually, intellectually, emotionally, physically, relationally, and sexually that we call evil "good" and we call good "evil" (Isaiah 5:20). David used the word *"iniquity"* in Psalm 51:5 and that word means to be bent towards evil and perversity. Therefore, some people are born bent towards homosexuality and homosexual tendencies. This is where God comes in because He can make that which is bent and crooked straight again or straight for the first time (Proverbs 3:5-6).

There are also demonic influences that contribute to homosexuality. The Bible says in Ephesians 6:10-12 that we wrestle against demons and these demons are arranged in military ranks and they have specific plans and assignments. Jesus once called a demon a *"deaf and dumb spirit"* implying that there are different kinds of demons (Mark 9:25). There are *"spirits of harlotry"* mentioned in the Scriptures (Hosea 4:12, 5:4), therefore it is not far fetched to believe that there are demons of homosexual oppressiveness that are assigned to people in order to influence them and destroy them (John 10:10).

There are generational curses that also contribute to the quality of our lives. Children are often punished because of the sins of their fathers (Exodus 20:4-6). In other words, kids reap what their parents' sow. What did your grandfather expose himself to that is visiting you and his other grandchildren? What sins are you given to because of the choices of your parents? Take the time to observe the sexual tendencies in your family tree. What King David did in moderation (II Samuel 3:2-5) King Solomon did in excess when it came to sexual perversion (I Kings 11:1-3). Generational curses can only be broken by confessing the sins, repenting from the sins, renouncing the sins, and relying totally upon Christ Jesus as your Savior and Lord (Proverbs 28:13). Jesus was cursed on the cross (Galatians 3:13) on behalf of sinners so that those who trust Him might be blessed and covered with the righteousness of God (II Corinthians 5:21). It is categorically impossible for a Christian to be cursed once they understand who they are in relation to Christ.

Finally, there is divine judgment. There comes a point where God gives a person over to destruction that stubbornly refuses to receive the truth and repent. God gives them over to the destructive desires and lifestyle that they want but also know is wrong (Romans 1:24-31). There is no coming back once a person has been handed over by God. Their consciences are seared and they become spiritual reprobates.

Biblically speaking, it is not possible for a person to be born a homosexual. It is possible through the sinful nature we each inherited through the fall of Adam and Eve, and through various societal, familial, and spiritual influences to be born with a bent towards homosexuality. Regardless of what kind of sin we were born with a bent towards, or what kind of sin we were exposed to in our youth, God has made provision for us to be born again with the divine capability to walk in freedom. Once again it is through repentance from sin, salvation in Jesus Christ, ongoing sanctification of the Holy Spirit, steadfast accountability, renouncing of spiritual darkness, and submission to professional, Christian counseling that God heals people overtaken by the sin homosexuality. The reality is that even with Jesus in your life, the struggles, urges and temptations for homosexual activity may never leave you completely, but through the empowering of the Holy Spirit you don't have to act on those urges.

By counseling with men and women in my church that have admitted to having homosexual and lesbian desires, I have grown more sensitive to how I serve them and publicly address this matter. I can't bash them or trash them. I have to reach them and teach them. As my compassion has grown, my wisdom has grown as well. If the church is going to make a difference in these last days and times, we have to be ready to properly face the homosexual quandary. Some of my men struggle with these illicit inclinations because of what past molestation at the hands of a "trusted" relative or friend brought upon them. We never use this information as an excuse. We use it to aid our understanding and increase our sympathy.

My Family Pastor, Daryl Fitzgerald, regularly walks men and women through the "Steps of Freedom" developed by Dr. Neil T. Anderson. Dr. Anderson is currently mentoring Pastor Daryl with these biblical principles and we are seeing life- changing fruit appear in our church. Our men are healthily bonding by confessing their faults to one another and praying for one another (James 5:16). I try to model a kind of transparency as the senior pastor that invites other men to be honest with God, themselves, and one another. We are discovering that many men want to be free and honest. They just need to know there are men in church they can talk to about it without being stoned. When this happens, a healed church can successfully reach a hurting and confused world.

GOD'S DIVERSE KINGDOM COME THROUGH **ONENESS**

"…for you are all one in Christ Jesus." Galatians 3:28d

1. THE ANSWER

"I do not pray for these alone, but also for those who will believe in Me through their word; that they all may be one, as You, Father, are in Me, and I in You: that they may also be one in Us, that the world may believe that You sent Me." John 17:20-21

Oneness is so important to the heart and program of God that it consumed the final prayer of Jesus Christ before His death by crucifixion. This prayer in the garden of Gethsemane has been called "The High Priestly Prayer" (John 17:1-26). In this supplication Jesus intercedes for His followers the way the high priest of old interceded to God in the temple on behalf of the Jewish people. As our Great High Priest, Jesus stood between God and the people and represented the interests of both towards the other as only He could (I Timothy 2:5, Hebrews 4:14-15). He represented God to the people and the people to God by being the only Person capable of putting His hands on both (Job 9:32-34).

Jesus covered thousands of years and billions of people in this prayer. Before He would pay for our sins on the cross, He prayed for our oneness as a result of the cross (John 12:32). His heart was tremendously burdened for how His followers would get along in the wake of His physical absence. If Jesus was burdened for this kind of unity, what should we be burdened for? If Jesus prayed for oneness, what should we pray for? What should we be about? The overriding theme of His heart's cry to God was for His followers then and now, red, brown, yellow, black and white, rich and poor, male and female to experience true oneness like He has with His Father (John 17:11, 21, 22, 23).

Just as love does (John 13:35), oneness amongst the redeemed children of God has a way of communicating to unbelievers the realty of Jesus Christ. Jesus is seen best when love and unity are being modeled among His spiritually adopted children. A lost and unbelieving world is moved more by what they see in us as opposed to what they hear from us. More is caught than taught when our actions speak louder than our words. If we love God we'll love our neighbor. If we love our neighbor regardless of race, class, or gender, the world will believe that Jesus Christ is who He said He was, and that is, the answer (John 14:6). What good is God if His love and His gospel can't bring Christians together? What good is Jesus if He is not capable of unifying His family on earth? Who wants to become a part of a divided, defeated, and dysfunctional family? But when a family is loving, and accepting, and places value on each member, people line up to become a part of it. They will gladly and proudly tell all kinds of people about their family and invite them to take part.

DO YOU KNOW THE ANSWER?

Jesus started this prayer to the Father by saying, *"And this is eternal life, that they may know You, the only true God, and Jesus Christ whom you have sent"* (John 17:3). Two things are significant in this one statement. One, eternal life is found in knowing God through Jesus Christ. Secondly, there is only one true God. As you read this prayer you will quickly be reminded that this one God is for the unity of His people. Oneness or unity is the answer to showing a lost world that what we preach to them truly works for us. When followers of Christ tell unbelievers that God's love can change them they want to know if God's love has changed us. Jesus is the only answer for the lost, but is He the only answer for the saved? Let's find out.

If I were to ask you to give me an addition equation that equaled the sum total of four you would say, "Two plus two equals four", and you would be correct. However, you would be in error if you said two plus two was the only way to equal the answer four. Why is that? There are many ways to get to the one, correct answer. Your republican neighbor across the street would say, "One plus one plus one plus one equals four", and he would be correct. Then the affluent businesswoman next door to you would say, "I also have an addition equation that equals four! Three plus one adds up to four." She would be correct. An intelligent, homeless man would say, "Wait a minute. Two plus one plus one, equal four." A Presbyterian pastor would chime in saying, "Four plus zero equals four." All of these people are correct. There are many different ways to get to the one answer, four.

Baptists may add things up a little differently than Pentecostals but they have the same answer, Jesus. In their equation, Latinos may have different things to consider than their Asian brothers and sisters, but they all have the same bottom line, Jesus. Women and men may use contrasting calculations but we both have the same conclusion, Christ. The wealthy and the not so wealthy may add things up with different numbers but ultimately they have the same sum, Jesus, the Son of God. There are many different ways to get to Jesus, the one and only answer. Just be sure to get to Him.

THE ANSWER IS "FOR"...

*"**FOR** God so loved the world that He gave His only begotten Son, that whoever believes in Him should not perish but have everlasting life."* John 3:16

*"**FOR** God did not send His Son into the world to condemn the world, but that the world through Him might be saved."* John 3:17

*"**FOR** by grace you have been saved through faith, and that not of yourselves; it is the gift of God, not of works, lest anyone should boast."* Ephesians 2:8-9

*"**FOR** we are His workmanship, created in Christ Jesus for good works, which God prepared beforehand that we should walk in them."* Ephesians 2:10

*"**FOR** there is one God and one Mediator between God and men, the Man Christ Jesus, who gave Himself a ransom for all..."* I Timothy 2:5-6

*"**FOR** there is no other name under heaven given among men by which we must be saved."* Acts 4:12

*"**FOR** our God is a consuming fire."* Hebrews 12:29

*"**FOR** God has highly exalted Him and given Him the name which is above every name, that at the name of Jesus every knee should bow, of those in heaven, and of those on the earth, and those under the earth, and that every tongue should confess that Jesus Christ is Lord, to the glory of God the Father."* Philippians 2:9-11

*"**FOR** by one Spirit we were all baptized into one body—whether Jews or Greeks, whether slaves or free—and have all been made to drink into one Spirit."* I Corinthians 12:13

*"**FOR** as many of you were baptized into Christ have put on Christ. There is neither Jew nor Greek, there is neither slave nor free, there is neither male nor female; for you are all one in Christ Jesus.* Galatians 3:27-28

WILL YOU BE THE ANSWER?

Christians know the answer. It's time to start with the same answer and work our way backwards. The world isn't seeing Jesus through us because we aren't together. His children are too busy bickering over politics, denominations, class, and race to gather together around the Son of God, Jesus Christ. Like never before we must pray for God's Diverse Kingdom to come on earth as it is in heaven. We shouldn't have to wait to go to heaven to have this unity. We shouldn't have to wait to die to know diversity the way God intended. We shouldn't have to wait to go to glory to experience the glory of blessed, Christian community.

And for some of us we're not going to wait. For some of us we refuse to wait. A holy indignation is stirring in us right now whereby we can't wait until heaven to experience heaven. We want heaven now and once you get a taste of God's Diverse Kingdom through what the Holy Spirit does (Romans 8:23), that small sample leaves you wanting more and more.

When Jesus prayed for oneness among His children He was praying for you and for me. As we have stated throughout this book, oneness does not mean sameness or the loss of identity. Oneness does not mean we will agree on every detail; however, oneness means that we will stand together, worship together, pray together, fight together, learn together, and minister together no matter what. Oneness means that we agree to disagree on secondary matters without being disagreeable. Oneness means that we will be people of blessed balance, depending upon God's Spirit to keep us perpendicular. Oneness means that our relationship with God through Jesus Christ rightfully supersedes our race, class, and gender, and this identity in Christ gives us the grace to subsequently view and healthily dialogue on matters of race, class, and gender.

I am the answer to Jesus' prayer for oneness. He saw me that day in the garden two thousand years ago in His mighty mind's eye. He prayed for me and I am so glad He did, therefore I personally refuse to be divided and separated over petty nonsense that has no eternal significance. Jesus' words to the Father will not be wasted as far as I am concerned. He was serious about oneness and so am I. I intend to live my life in such a way that lost people will see Jesus through me. They will see Him by how I love and unite with others who are not like me. I will not allow differences to bring division any longer. I choose to celebrate our appropriate differences and learn from them. Jesus prayed for me and His prayers for unity will not go unanswered in me. I am the answer to His prayer for oneness and I will represent Him and His Diverse Kingdom on earth.

What about you? Will you stand with us in God's Diverse Kingdom?